PRAYERS FROM PRISON

PRAYERS FROM PRISON

PRAYERS AND POEMS

Dietrich Bonhoeffer

Interpreted by
JOHANN CHRISTOPH HAMPE

FORTRESS PRESS
Philadelphia

First published as Dietrich Bonhoeffer, *Von guten Mächten: Gebete und Gedichte,* interpretiert von Johann Christoph Hampe © 1976 by Chr. Kaiser Verlag, Munich.

Selections from *Letters and Papers from Prison* are reprinted by arrangement with Macmillan Publishing Co., Inc. Copyright © 1953, 1967, 1971 by SCM Press, Ltd.

"Night Voices in Tegel." From *I Loved This People* by Dietrich Bonhoeffer. © M. E. Bratcher 1965. Used by permission of John Knox Press.

"Friday's Child." Copyright © 1958 by W. H. Auden. Reprinted from *Collected Poems,* by W. H. Auden, edited by Edward Mendelson, by permission of Random House, Inc.

The remaining material is translated by John Bowden.

First American Edition by Fortress Press 1978

Commentary copyright © 1977 in the English translation by William Collins Sons & Co. Ltd., London

Library of Congress Cataloging in Publication Data

Bonhoeffer, Dietrich, 1906-1945.
   Prayers from prison.

   Translation of Von guten Mächten.
   Includes bibliographical references.
   I. Hampe, Johann Christoph, 1913-   II. Title
PT2603.062V613   1978   831'.9'12   77-15228
ISBN 0-8006-1334-1

6502K77   Printed in the United States of America   1-1334

CONTENTS

PRAYERS FOR FELLOW-PRISONERS

MORNING PRAYERS

O God, early in the morning I cry to you.
Help me to pray
And to concentrate my thoughts on you;
I cannot do this alone.

In me there is darkness,
But with you there is light;
I am lonely, but you do not leave me;
I am feeble in heart, but with you there is help;
I am restless, but with you there is peace.
In me there is bitterness, but with you there is patience;
I do not understand your ways,
But you know the way for me.

O heavenly Father,
I praise and thank you
For the peace of the night;
I praise and thank you for this new day;
I praise and thank you for all your goodness
and faithfulness throughout my life.

You have granted me many blessings;
Now let me also accept what is hard
from your hand.
You will lay on me no more
than I can bear.
You make all things work together for good
for your children.

Lord Jesus Christ,
You were poor
and in distress, a captive and forsaken as I am.
You know all man's troubles;

7

You abide with me
when all men fail me;
You remember and seek me;
It is your will that I should know you
and turn to you.
Lord, I hear your call and follow;
Help me.

O Holy Spirit,
Give me faith that will protect me
from despair, from passions, and from vice;
Give me such love for God and men
as will blot out all hatred and bitterness;
Give me the hope that will deliver me
from fear and faint-heartedness.

O holy and merciful God,
my Creator and Redeemer,
my Judge and Saviour,
You know me and all that I do.
You hate and punish evil without respect of persons
in this world and the next;
You forgive the sins of those
who sincerely pray for forgiveness;
You love goodness, and reward it on this earth
with a clear conscience,
and, in the world to come,
with a crown of righteousness.

I remember in your presence all my loved ones,
my fellow-prisoners, and all who in this house
perform their hard service;
Lord, have mercy.

Restore me to liberty,
and enable me so to live now
that I may answer before you and before men.

Lord, whatever this day may bring,
Your name be praised.
Amen.

In my sleep he watches yearning
and restores my soul,
so that each recurring morning
love and goodness make me whole.
Were God not there,
his face not near,
He had not led me out of fear.
All things have their time and sphere:
God's love lasts for ever.

Paul Gerhardt

EVENING PRAYERS

O Lord my God, thank you
for bringing this day to a close;
Thank you for giving me rest
in body and soul.
Your hand has been over me
and has guarded and preserved me.
Forgive my lack of faith
and any wrong that I have done today,
and help me to forgive all who have wronged me.

Let me sleep in peace under your protection,
and keep me from all the temptations of darkness.

Into your hands I commend my loved ones
and all who dwell in this house;

I commend to you my body and soul.
O God, your holy name be praised.
Amen.

Each day tells the other
my life is but a journey
to great and endless life.
O sweetness of eternity,
may my heart grow to love thee;
my home is not in time's strife.

Tersteegen

Prayers in time of Distress

O Lord God,
great distress has come upon me;
my cares threaten to crush me,
and I do not know what to do.
O God, be gracious to me and help me.
Give me strength to bear what you send,
and do not let fear rule over me;
Take a father's care of my wife and children.

O merciful God,
forgive me all the sins that I have committed
against you and against my fellow men.
I trust in your grace
and commit my life wholly into your hands.
Do with me according to your will
and as is best for me.
Whether I live or die, I am with you,
and you, my God, are with me.
Lord, I wait for your salvation
and for your kingdom.
Amen.

Every Christian in his place
should be brave and free,
with the world face to face.
Though death strikes, his spirit should
persevere, without fear
calm and good.

For death cannot destroy,
but from grief brings relief
and opens gates to joy.
Closed the door of bitter pain,
bright the way where we may
all heaven gain.

Paul Gerhardt

November 1943

THE PAST

O happiness beloved, and pain beloved in heaviness,
you went from me.
What shall I call you? Anguish, life, blessedness,
part of myself, my heart – the past?
The door was slammed;
I hear your steps depart and slowly die away.
What now remains for me – torment, delight, desire?
This only do I know: that with you, all has gone.
But do you feel how I now grasp at you
and so clutch hold of you
that it must hurt you?
How I so rend you
that your blood gushes out,
simply to be sure that you are near me,
a life in earthly form, complete?
Do you divine my terrible desire
for my own suffering,
my eager wish to see my own blood flow,
only that all may not go under,
lost in the past?

Life, what have you done to me?
Why did you come? Why did you go?
Past, when you flee from me,
are you not still my past, my own?
As o'er the sea the sun sinks ever faster,
as if it moved towards the darkness,
so does your image sink and sink and sink
without a pause
into the ocean of the past,
and waves engulf it.
As the warm breath dissolves
in the cool morning air,
so does your image vanish from me,
and I forget your face, your hands, your form.
There comes a smile, a glance, a greeting;

it fades, dissolves,
comfortless, distant,
is destroyed, is past.

I would inhale the fragrance of your being,
absorb it, stay with it,
as on hot summer days the heavy blossoms welcoming the
bees intoxicate them,
as privet makes the hawk-moths drunken –
but a harsh gust destroys both scent and blossoms,
and I stand like a fool
seeking a past that vanished.

It is as if parts of my flesh were torn out with red-hot pincers,
when you, a part of my life that is past, so quickly depart.
Raging defiance and anger beset me,
reckless and profitless questions I fling into space.
'Why, why, why?' I keep on repeating –
why cannot my senses hold you,
life now passing, now past?
Thus I will think, and think anew,
until I find what I have lost.

But I feel
that everything around me, over, under me
is smiling at me, unmoved, enigmatic,
smiling at my hopeless efforts
to grasp the wind,
to capture what has gone.

Evil comes into my eye and soul;
what I see, I hate;
I hate what moves me;
all that lives I hate, all that is lovely,
all that would recompense me for my loss.
I want my life; I claim my own life back again,
my past, yourself.
Yourself. A tear wells up and fills my eye;

can I, in mists of tears,
regain your image,
yourself entire?
But I will not weep;
only the strong are helped by tears,
weaklings they make ill.

Wearily I come to the evening;
welcome are bed and oblivion
now that my own is denied me.
Night, blot out what separates, give me oblivion,
in charity perform your kindly office;
to you I trust myself.
But night is wise and mighty,
wiser than I, and mightier than day.
What no earthly power can do,
what is denied to thoughts and senses, to defiance, to tears,
night brings me, in its bounty overflowing.
Unharmed by hostile time,
pure, free, and whole,
you are brought to me by dream,
you, my past, my life,
you, the day and hour but lately gone.

Close to you I waken in the dead of night,
and start with fear –
are you lost to me once more? Is it always vainly that I seek
you, you, my past?
I stretch my hands out,
and I pray –
and a new thing now I hear:
'The past will come to you once more,
and be your life's enduring part,
through thanks and repentance.
Feel in the past God's forgiveness and goodness,
pray him to keep you today and tomorrow.'

June 1944

SORROW AND JOY

Sorrow and joy,
striking suddenly on our startled senses,
seem, at the first approach, all but impossible
of just distinction one from the other,
even as frost and heat at the first keen contact
burn us alike.

Joy and sorrow,
hurled from the height of heaven in meteor fashion,
flash in an arc of shining menace o'er us.
Those they touch are left
stricken amid the fragments
of their colourless, usual lives.

Imperturbable, mighty,
ruinous and compelling,
sorrow and joy
– summoned or all unsought for –
processionally enter.
Those they encounter
they transfigure, investing them
with strange gravity
and a spirit of worship.

Joy is rich in fears;
sorrow has its sweetness.
Indistinguishable from each other
they approach us from eternity,
equally potent in their power and terror.

From every quarter
mortals come hurrying,
part envious, part awe-struck,
swarming, and peering
into the portent,

where the mystery sent from above us
is transmuting into the inevitable
order of earthly human drama.

What, then, is joy? What, then, is sorrow?
Time alone can decide between them,
when the immediate poignant happening
lengthens out to continuous wearisome suffering,
when the laboured creeping moments of daylight
slowly uncover the fullness of our disaster,
sorrow's unmistakable features.

Then do most of our kind,
sated, if only by the monotony
of unrelieved unhappiness,
turn away from the drama, disillusioned,
uncompassionate.

O you mothers and loved ones – then, ah, then
comes your hour, the hour for true devotion.
Then your hour comes, you friends and brothers!
Loyal hearts can change the face of sorrow,
softly encircle it with love's most gentle
unearthly radiance.

June 1944

WHO AM I?

Who am I? They often tell me
I would step from my cell's confinement
calmly, cheerfully, firmly,
like a squire from his country house.

Who am I? They often tell me
I would talk to my warders
freely and friendly and clearly,
as though it were mine to command.

Who am I? They also tell me
I would bear the days of misfortune
equably, smilingly, proudly,
like one accustomed to win.

Am I then really all that which other men tell of?
Or am I only what I know of myself,
restless and longing and sick, like a bird in a cage,
struggling for breath, as though hands were compressing my
    throat,
yearning for colours, for flowers, for the voices of birds,
thirsting for words of kindness, for neighbourliness,
trembling with anger at despotisms and petty humiliation,
tossing in expectation of great events,
powerlessly trembling for friends at an infinite distance,
weary and empty at praying, at thinking, at making,
faint, and ready to say farewell to it all?

Who am I? This or the other?
Am I one person today, and tomorrow another?
Am I both at once? A hypocrite before others,
and before myself a contemptibly woebegone weakling?
Or is something within me still like a beaten army,
fleeing in disorder from victory already achieved?

Who am I? They mock me, these lonely questions of mine.
Whoever I am, thou knowest, O God, I am thine.

June 1944

NIGHT VOICES IN TEGEL

Stretched out on my cot
I stare at the grey wall.
Outside, a summer evening
That does not know me
Goes singing into the countryside.
Slowly and softly
The tides of the day ebb
On the eternal shore.
Sleep a little,
Strengthen body and soul, head and hand,
For peoples, houses, spirits and hearts
Are aflame.
Till your day breaks
After blood-red night –
Stand fast!

Night and silence.
I listen.
Only the steps and cries of the guards,
The distant, hidden laughter of two lovers.
Do you hear nothing else, lazy sleeper?

I hear my own soul tremble and heave.
Nothing else?
I hear, I hear
The silent night thoughts
Of my fellow sufferers asleep or awake,
As if voices, cries,
As if shouts for planks to save them.
I hear the uneasy creak of the beds,
I hear chains.

I hear how sleepless men toss and turn,
Who long for freedom and deeds of wrath.
When at grey dawn sleep finds them
They murmur in dreams of their wives and children.

I hear the happy lisp of half-grown boys,
Delighting in childhood dreams;
I hear them tug at their blankets
And hide from hideous nightmares.

I hear the sighs and weak breath of the old,
Who in silence prepare for the last journey.
They have seen justice and injustice come and go;
Now they wish to see the imperishable, the eternal.

Night and silence.
Only the steps and cries of the guards.
Do you hear how in the silent house
It quakes, cracks, roars
When hundreds kindle the stirred-up flame of their hearts?

Their choir is silent,
But my ear is open wide:
'We the old, the young,
The sons of all tongues,
We the strong, the weak,
The sleepers, the wakeful,
We the poor, the rich,
Alike in misfortune,
The good, the bad,
Whatever we have been,
We men of many scars,
We the witnesses of those who died,
We the defiant, we the despondent,
The innocent, and the much accused,
Deeply tormented by long isolation,
Brother, we are searching, we are calling you!
Brother, do you hear me?'

Twelve cold, thin strokes of the tower clock
Awaken me.
No sound, no warmth in them
To hide and cover me.

Howling, evil dogs at midnight
Frighten me.
The wretched noise
Divides a poor yesterday
From a poor today.
What can it matter to me
Whether one day turns into another,
One that could have nothing new, nothing better
Than to end quickly like this one?
I want to see the turning of the times,

When luminous signs stand in the night sky,
And over the peoples new bells
Ring and ring.
I am waiting for that midnight
In whose fearfully streaming brilliance
The evil perish for anguish
And the good overcome with joy.

The villain
Comes to light
In the judgement.

Deceit and betrayal,
Malicious deeds –
Atonement is near.

See, O man,
Holy strength
Is at work, setting right.

Rejoice and proclaim
Faithfulness and right
For a new race!

Heaven, reconcile
The sons of earth
To peace and beauty.

Earth, flourish;
Man, become free,
Be free!

Suddenly I sat up,
As if, from a sinking ship, I had sighted land,
As if there were something to grasp, to seize,
As if I saw golden fruit ripen.
But wherever I look, grasp, or seize,
There is only the impenetrable mass of darkness.

I sink into brooding;
I sink myself into the depths of the dark.
You night, full of outrage and evil,
Make yourself known to me!
Why and for how long will you try our patience?
A deep and long silence;
Then I hear the night bend down to me:
'I am not dark; only guilt is dark!'

Guilt! I hear a trembling and quaking,
A murmur, a lament that arises;
I hear men grow angry in spirit.
In the wild uproar of innumerable voices
A silent chorus
Assails God's ear:

'Pursued and hunted by men,
Made defenceless and accused,
Bearers of unbearable burdens,
We are yet the accusers.

'We accuse those who plunged us into sin,
Who made us share the guilt,
Who made us the witnesses of injustice,
In order to despise their accomplices.

'Our eyes had to see folly,
In order to bind us in deep guilt;
Then they stopped our mouths,
And we were as dumb dogs.

'We learned to lie easily,
To be at the disposal of open injustice;
If the defenceless was abused,
Then our eyes remained cold.

'And that which burned in our hearts,
Remained silent and unnamed;
We quenched our fiery blood
And stamped out the inner flame.

'The once holy bonds uniting men
Were mangled and flayed,
Friendship and faithfulness betrayed;
Tears and rue were reviled.

'We sons of pious races,
One-time defenders of right and truth,
Became despisers of God and man,
Amid hellish laughter.

'Yet though now robbed of freedom and honour,
We raise our heads proudly before men.
And if we are brought into disrepute,
Before men we declare our innocence.

'Steady and firm we stand man against man;
As the accused we accuse!

'Only before thee, source of all being,
Before thee are we sinners.

'Afraid of suffering and poor in deeds,
We have betrayed thee before men.

'We saw the lie raise its head,
And we did not honour the truth.

'We saw brethren in direst need,
And feared only our own death.

'We come before thee as men,
As confessors of our sins.

'Lord, after the ferment of these times,
Send us times of assurance.

'After so much going astray,
Let us see the day break.

'Let there be ways built for us by thy word
As far as eye can see.

'Until thou wipe out our guilt,
Keep us in quiet patience.

'We will silently prepare ourselves,
Till thou dost call to new times.

'Until thou stillest storm and flood,
And thy will does wonders.

'Brother, till the night be past,
Pray for me!'

The first light of morning creeps through my window pale
    and grey,
A light, warm summer wind blows over my brow.
'Summer day,' I will only say, 'beautiful summer day!'
What may it bring to me?
Then I hear outside hasty, muffled steps;
Near me they stop suddenly.
I turn cold and hot,

For I know, oh, I know!
A soft voice reads something cuttingly and cold.
Control yourself, brother; soon you will have finished it,
soon, soon.
I hear you stride bravely and with proud step.
You no longer see the present, you see the future.
I go with you, brother, to that place,
And I hear your last word:
'Brother, when the sun turns pale for me,
Then live for me.'

Stretched out on my cot
I stare at the grey wall.
Outside a summer morning
Which is not yet mine
Goes brightly into the countryside.

Brother, till after the long night
Our day breaks
We stand fast!

June 1944

CHRISTIANS AND PAGANS

1

Men go to God when they are sore bestead,
Pray to him for succour, for his peace, for bread,
For mercy for them sick, sinning, or dead;
All men do so, Christian and unbelieving.

2

Men go to God when he is sore bestead,
Find him poor and scorned, without shelter or bread,
Whelmed under weight of the wicked, the weak, the dead;
Christians stand by God in his hour of grieving.

3

God goes to every man when sore bestead,
Feeds body and spirit with his bread;
For Christians, pagans alike he hangs dead,
And both alike forgiving.

July 1944

STATIONS ON THE ROAD TO FREEDOM

DISCIPLINE

If you set out to seek freedom, then learn above all things
to govern your soul and your senses, for fear that your passions
and longing may lead you away from the path you should
   follow.
Chaste be your mind and your body, and both in subjection,
obediently, steadfastly seeking the aim set before them;
only through discipline may a man learn to be free.

ACTION

Daring to do what is right, not what fancy may tell you,
valiantly grasping occasions, not cravenly doubting —
freedom comes only through deeds, not through thoughts
   taking wing.
Faint not nor fear, but go out to the storm and the action,
trusting in God whose commandment you faithfully follow;
freedom, exultant, will welcome your spirit with joy.

SUFFERING

A change has come indeed. Your hands, so strong and active,
are bound; in helplessness now you see your action
is ended; you sigh in relief, your cause committing
to stronger hands; so now you may rest contented.
Only for one blissful moment could you draw near to touch
   freedom;
then, that it might be perfected in glory, you gave it to God.

DEATH

Come now, thou greatest of feasts on the journey to freedom
   eternal;
death, cast aside all the burdensome chains, and demolish

the walls of our temporal body, the walls of our souls that are
   blinded,
so that at last we may see that which here remains hidden.
Freedom, how long we have sought thee in discipline, action,
   and suffering;
dying, we now may behold thee revealed in the Lord.

July 1944

THE FRIEND

Not from the heavy soil,
where blood and sex and oath
rule in their hallowed might,
where earth itself,
guarding the primal consecrated order,
avenges wantonness and madness –
not from the heavy soil of earth,
but from the spirit's choice and free desire,
needing no oath or legal bond,
is friend bestowed on friend.

Beside the cornfield that sustains us,
tilled and cared for reverently by men
sweating as they labour at their task,
and, if need be, giving their life's blood –
beside the field that gives their daily bread
men also let the lovely cornflower thrive.
No one has planted, no one watered it;
it grows, defenceless and in freedom,
and in glad confidence of life untroubled
under the open sky.
Beside the staff of life,
taken and fashioned from the heavy earth,
beside our marriage, work, and war,
the free man, too, will live and grow towards the sun.
Not the ripe fruit alone –
blossom is lovely, too.
Does blossom only serve the fruit,
or does fruit only serve the blossom –
who knows?
But both are given to us.
Finest and rarest blossom,
at a happy moment springing
from the freedom of a lightsome, daring, trusting spirit,
is a friend to a friend.

Playmates at first
on the spirit's long journeys
to distant and wonderful realms
that, veiled by the morning sunlight,
glitter like gold;
when, in the midday heat
the gossamer clouds in the deep blue sky
drift slowly towards them –
realms that, when night stirs the senses,
lit by the lamps in the darkness,
like treasures prudently hidden
beckon the seeker.

When the spirit touches
man's heart and brow
with thoughts that are lofty, bold, serene,
so that with clear eyes he will face the world
as a free man may;
when then the spirit gives birth to action
by which alone we stand or fall;
when from the sane and resolute action
rises the work that gives a man's life
content and meaning –
then would that man,
lonely and actively working,
know of the spirit that grasps and befriends him,
like waters clear and refreshing
where the spirit is cleansed from the dust
and cooled from the heat that oppressed him,
steeling himself in the hour of fatigue –
like a fortress to which, from confusion and danger,
the spirit returns,
wherein he finds refuge and comfort and strengthening,
is a friend to a friend.

And the spirit will trust,
trust without limit.

Sickened by vermin
that feed, in the shade of the good,
on envy, greed, and suspicion,
by the snake-like hissing
of venomous tongues
that fear and hate and revile
the mystery of free thought
and upright heart,
the spirit would cast aside all deceit,
open his heart to the spirit he trusts,
and unite with him freely as one.
Ungrudging, he will support,
will thank and acknowledge him,
and from him draw happiness and strength.

But always to rigorous
judgement and censure
freely assenting,
man seeks, in his manhood,
not orders, not laws and peremptory dogmas,
but counsel from one who is earnest in goodness
and faithful in friendship,
making man free.

Distant or near,
in joy or in sorrow,
each in the other
sees his true helper
to brotherly freedom.

At midnight came the air-raid siren's song;
I thought of you in silence and for long –
how you are faring, how our lives once were,
and how I wish you home this coming year.

We wait till half past one, and hear at last
the signal that the danger now is past;

so danger – if the omen does not lie –
of every kind shall gently pass you by.

August 1944

THE DEATH OF MOSES

Deuteronomy 34:1: And the Lord showed him all the land

Upon the mountain's summit stands at last
Moses, the prophet and the man of God.

Unwavering his eyes look on the view,
survey the promised scene, the holy land.

'Now, Lord, thy promises have been fulfilled,
to me thy word has been for ever sure.

Deliverance and salvation are thy gifts,
thy anger chastens, casts away, consumes.

Eternal faithful Lord, thy faithless slave
knows well – at all times righteous is thy will.

So now, today, inflict my punishment,
enfold me in the long dark sleep of death.

Rich grow the vineyards in the holy land;
faith only knows the promise of their wine.

Pour for the doubter, then, his bitter draught,
and let his faith proclaim thy thanks and praise.

Wondrous the works which thou hast done by me,
changing my cup from gall to sweet delight.

Grant me to witness through the veil of death
my people at their high triumphant feast.

I fail, and sink in thine eternity,
but see my people marching forward, free.

God, quick to punish sin or to forgive,
thou knowest how this people has my love.

Enough that I have borne its shame and sin
and seen salvation – now I need not live.

Stay, hold my nerveless hands, let fall my staff;
thou faithful God, prepare for me my grave.'

September 1944

almost two years which he was compelled to spend in
[Hit]ler's prisons. He was executed on 9 April 1945, after
[sen]tence had been passed on him by a hastily summoned
[em]ergency court, but until that time he had merely been
[det]ained for questioning: formally, he had the rights of a
[cit]izen, and sometimes these had been respected. During
[the]se last months he at least had time. He was disciplined
[en]ough to use it for indefatigable reading and extensive
[wr]iting. During these oppressive months he gave us of his
[be]st: it was smuggled out and brought to safety piece by
[pi]ece by his friend Eberhard Bethge and his relatives. It was
[h]is best, although because of the disturbed times and the
[w]ealth of perspectives opening up to him it was presented as
[s]ketches, outlines, raw material. His letters suggest plans for
[e]ntire books, asking questions to which he could find no re-
[p]lies in his prison cell. This is the category into which his
[p]oems also fall.

The foundation for his literary interests and for his own
later efforts had already been laid at home. Karl Bonhoeffer
was a psychiatrist who was highly respected by his colleagues.
In Breslau and Berlin the family, with eight children and
numerous interested relatives, made up an open circle which
was much more interested in intellectual and cultural
matters than questions of business and commerce. At an
early age Dietrich Bonhoeffer grew accustomed to the best of
the middle-class culture of his time. People felt at home in the
world of the German classics and the music of the nine-
teenth century. To Dietrich's father, clichés were anathema.
Once its spiritual sickness had been recognized, National
Socialism was not even a matter for discussion. Conservatism
in questions of nationalism, as well as a liberal attitude,
formed the basis for the Bonhoeffers' resistance. Dietrich's
earlier decision to study theology had come as a surprise,
but it was accepted nevertheless. It was impossible for him to
break away from home, and throughout his life the links
were maintained, to his benefit.

In all this, his literary efforts played their part – not only
his poems, but the fragments of plays and novels which were

JONAH

In fear of death they cried aloud and, clinging fast
to wet ropes straining on the battered deck,
they gazed in stricken terror at the sea
that now, unchained in sudden fury, lashed the ship.

'O gods eternal, excellent, provoked to anger,
help us, or give a sign, that we may know
who has offended you by secret sin,
by breach of oath, or heedless blasphemy, or murder,

who brings us to disaster by misdeed still hidden,
to make a paltry profit for his pride.'
Thus they besought. And Jonah said, 'Behold,
I sinned before the Lord of hosts. My life is forfeit.

Cast me away! My guilt must bear the wrath of God;
the righteous shall not perish with the sinner!'
They trembled. But with hands that knew no weakness
they cast the offender from their midst. The sea stood still.

October 1944

POWERS OF GOOD

With every power for good to stay and guide me,
comforted and inspired beyond all fear,
I'll live these days with you in thought beside me,
and pass, with you, into the coming year.

The old year still torments our hearts, unhastening;
the long days of our sorrow still endure;
Father, grant to the souls thou hast been chastening
that thou hast promised, the healing and the cure.

Should it be ours to drain the cup of grieving
even to the dregs of pain, at thy command,
we will not falter, thankfully receiving
all that is given by thy loving hand.

But should it be thy will once more to release us
to life's enjoyment and its good sunshine,
that which we've learned from sorrow shall increase us,
and all our life be dedicate as thine.

Today, let candles shed their radiant greeting;
lo, on our darkness are they not thy light
leading us, haply, to our longed-for meeting? –
Thou canst illumine even our darkest night.

When now the silence deepens for our hearkening,
grant we may hear thy children's voices raise
from all the unseen world around us darkening
their universal paean, in thy praise.

While all the powers of good aid and attend us,
boldly we'll face the future, come what may.
At even and at morn God will befriend us,
and oh, most surely on each newborn day!

December 1944

AN INTERPRETATIO

JOHANN CHRISTOPH HAMPE

The last year

This book contains eleven poems written
Bonhoeffer, and one about him by W. H. Aud
in 1973. These eleven poems are all of his that
and they all come from the time when he was in
had written poems in his youth, but this talent, lil
greater gifts in music-making, retreated into the b
in favour of his more important concern, his one g
life. Nevertheless, throughout his life he was a
reader. He read quickly and therefore assimilate
deal. His way of doing theology and his understa
theology and its content meant that he had as
approach to literature as possible, and did not wan
anything that was significant in the sphere of phil
history and literature if he could get hold of it. 1
particularly interested in stories, but less concerne
the secondary literature which proliferates in the huma
He was particularly keen to understand the hist
dimension.

Of course, men increasingly meant more to him than be
and he read voraciously in order to understand his cont
poraries better. After all, it was for them that he worke
theology and it was among them that he wanted to b
pastor. A master of serious conversation, cheerful banter a
letter-writing alike, he needed his contemporaries in ord
to understand himself. However, no man of any time can l
understood without his history. For Bonhoeffer, it was muc
more important to look back at historical conditioning thar
to make psychological investigations. He never lost his
awareness that the present had been shaped by the past.

The time when he was most engaged in literature and
when his reading was most extensive was during the period

published only in the most tentative form. The conservative traits in Dietrich Bonhoeffer's character should not be overlooked. His taste was never avant-garde, either in literature or in music. However, we should be very careful where we draw the line. Bonhoeffer was not the slightest bit interested in conservative efforts to preserve the past, either in his capacity as a theologian, as a man with political concerns, or simply as a human being. At any rate, as a theologian, he looked far into the future, even if he seems to have imagined that after Hitler, Germany would become above all a national entity with a Christian spirit. He was conservative for the simple reason that the only way in which he could think historically was in the light of the tradition of his ancient family; of the attitudes which had stood the test of time within it; and of his mature learning which made him look at both the letter and the spirit of remote times, as well as those nearer to his own.

Because of this, we should certainly expect the poetry of an imitator rather than that of a truly creative artist. Bonhoeffer was a long way from regarding himself as a poet (*LPP*, 372), and did not feel that he was in the happy position of being able to give poetic credibility to his verse by writing it in a distinctive form. It is always dominated by the desire to state something, to communicate an experience, and lacks the detachment of the true artist. In the *Letters and Papers from Prison* collected by Eberhard Bethge we sometimes find the content of prose texts expressed in verse. Thus all the elements of the poem 'Stations on the Road to Freedom' and virtually all its key phrases are also to be found in the letter of 28 July 1944. An integral part of our attempt to interpret these poems must therefore be to trace the key phrases in them through Bonhoeffer's thought. Nevertheless, quite independently of their very varied quality, the poems remain a necessary and independent testimony to their author's account of himself.

I am not referring here to the magic which is always to be found in poetry because it is an organized, contrived, concentrated form of expression. Something of this will remain even if the writer takes over a model from elsewhere, as Bonhoeffer does here when he imitates the style of Schiller, Hölderlin, C. F. Meyer, or that of the Expressionists from the generation of the First World War. We can let Bonhoeffer say in his own words what makes some of these poems – at least six of them – an indispensable part of his writing and profoundly satisfying works in their own right, as well as assuring them a place at the heart of Christianity for a long time to come. At one point in his letters from prison he discusses the difference between 'simplicity' and 'simpleness,' using Adalbert Stifter as an example. Taking up this distinction as Bonhoeffer uses it, I should like to say that in the move from prose to poetry Bonhoeffer's thoughts, which always have the character of simplicity, have gained simpleness. Simplicity is the prerequisite for profundity, the result of spiritual maturity. 'One can acquire "simplicity", but "simpleness" is innate.' In the poems Bonhoeffer is utterly himself. No more than this must be said about their significance. Bonhoeffer goes on: 'The two things seem to me to be related in much the same way as "purity" and "moderation". One can be "pure" only in relation to one's origin or goal, i.e. in relation to baptism or to forgiveness at the Lord's Supper; like "simpleness" it involves the idea of totality. If we have lost our purity – and we have all lost it – it can be given back to us in faith; but in ourselves, as living and developing persons, we can no longer be "pure" but only "moderate", and that is a possible and a necessary aim of education and culture' (*LPP*, 212). It may not have always been the case elsewhere in Bonhoeffer's life, but here in the poems purity includes moderation and simplicity includes simpleness. The poet may lament the loss of purity in his aristocratic approach to life and the loss of simpleness in his burdened conscience, but these qualities are to be found in the poems 'The Past', 'Sorrow and Joy', 'Who am I?', 'Christians and Pagans', 'Stations on the Road to Freedom', 'The Friend', 'Jonah' and 'Powers of Good'.

The history of literature shows us a wealth of archetypes of the poet. Dietrich Bonhoeffer, the man who did not mean to be a poet, the pastor executed among the 'godless' because the world, and not the church, needs God's witness, does not fit any of them. Was he a singer? Yes, he was that too. He could make music in the spirit even without an instrument and he could sing the psalms; he had composed music as a young man. Was he a priest? Yes, he was that too. Otherwise he would not have written about the sacrifice of Jonah. Was he a popular entertainer? Certainly not. But he knew how to play. He played chess on the day before his death. Was he a poor man? Money had no value for him; he had it and knew how to give it away. But he praised asceticism without becoming an ascetic. Was he a sufferer, like Dostoevsky and Hölderlin? He refused to allow people to call his imprisonment suffering. He celebrated suffering as 'a wondrous change' and death as the 'greatest of feasts on the journey to freedom eternal'. Did he turn his back on the world? Never, for his task was proclamation and assertion, not renunciation. But Adalbert Stifter, noted for his renunciation, was his friend, because he maintained detachment. Bonhoeffer was no magician with words, and as the fragment of his novel shows, his literary imagination had comparatively narrow limits. Taking the major compositions into account, his most prominent characteristic is that of a seer. In the few poems that he wrote he disclosed a corner of our future – and we should allow this to make its mark on us. The fact remains, that although today this young man would be seventy years old in fact his ashes lie in a mass grave. He saw what we long to be.

His poems will be the occasion for us to mention some of his ideas. At several points we shall be describing, quite briefly, the most important elements of what was important for him. His concern has been described at length elsewhere. It continues. It has a life of its own. His poems will be the occasion for us to tell of this one year during which they were composed, from Christmas 1943 to Christmas 1944. It was far richer than we can express. We shall hear something about the man – enough to give a background to the poems. No more, for he certainly would not have wished us to keep him company through 1945, that evil year, when he spoke his last words. We should remember them: 'This is the end – for me the beginning of life. . . . He ran quickly down the stairs,' wrote his biographer (*DB*, 830).

Bonhoeffer himself did not mean to be a poet, but a witness. Is not the witness more than the poet? Simpler, purer than he? And could any Christian be unaware that the word witness has a double meaning? Did he take our place? Not as Christ did – Bonhoeffer emphatically dismissed such an idea – but in his discipleship? 'We are not Christ's, but if we want to be Christians, we must have some share in Christ's large-heartedness by acting with responsibility and in freedom when the hour of danger comes, and by showing a real sympathy that springs, not from fear, but from the liberating and redeeming love of Christ for all who suffer' (*LPP*, 14).

Those words are taken from his reckoning 'After Ten Years', i.e. ten years after the beginning of Hitler's rule. His elderly parents hid these papers in the roof-beams of their house in Marienburger Allee, where the incendiary bombs – had they fallen – would have first caught hold. 'Death,' we read in a fragment of a play, 'is the standard for words.' Bonhoeffer puts this remark into the mouth of the impetuous young Christoph, who plays Bonhoeffer's own part in conversation and seeks 'to protect the great words which have been given to men from being misused' (*TP*, 198). His friend Bethge suggested that one great word might be deleted from the poem on friendship: the word 'lovely'. Is it not enough to call friendship a 'cornflower in the field'? Does it have to be a 'lovely cornflower'? One word, a little excessive. We read great poetry, but not great words. Its standard, death, peers in through the window.

Only one more thing concerns me. It might happen that in reading – and even better, as I would hope, in learning – these poems, we might follow a course that Dietrich Bonhoeffer certainly did not adopt. They begin with melancholy. They become more and more serious. 'The door was slammed.' We must also remember that the sequence of these poems from prison obeys a law to which we are all subject. It was the greatness of Dietrich Bonhoeffer that, as far as we can tell, he overcame this law and gained his freedom. Although his father was a psychiatrist, neither he nor Dietrich liked psychology. Yet the laws of psychology remained in force. And it is a demonstrable law of psychology that we have to let all our mourning have its course. Reading between the lines, one can see how between his arrest and his death Dietrich Bonhoeffer had to follow a course from the initial shock of imprisonment to resistance and dispute, from regression to acceptance. And who knows the phases? They saw him stepping from his cell like a 'squire', always open and in command, with so much in his gaze to pass on to others. But he knew better. He saw himself more clearly: 'Who am I?' He knew how he lay on his prison bed and argued with God.

The course on which he would not want us to embark in our thinking would be to regard him as a saint. He himself spoke out emphatically against this. In America, in conversation with a Frenchman, he had once said: 'I would not want to become a saint, but I should like to learn to have faith' (*LPP*, 369). For a long time he had not understood the profundity of this contrast. What is the meaning of faith? 'We must persevere in quiet meditation on the life, sayings, deeds, sufferings, and death of Jesus. It is certain that we may always live close to God and in the light of his presence, and that such living is an entirely new life for us; that nothing is then impossible for us, because all things are possible with God; that no earthly power can touch us without his will, and that danger and distress can only drive us closer to him. It is certain that we can claim nothing for ourselves, and may yet pray for everything: it is certain that our joy is hidden in suffering, and our life is death; it is certain that in all this we are in a fellowship that sustains us. In Jesus God has said Yes and Amen to it all, and that Yes and Amen is the firm ground on which we stand' (*LPP*, 391).

PRAYERS FOR FELLOW-PRISONERS

These texts have only been included among Bonhoeffer's literary efforts after some hesitation. Now, however, they come first in this collection. There are three reasons for this. None of the poems which follow arises so explicitly out of an immediate physical threat. Bonhoeffer was led to compose these prayers by his distress during the nights in December 1943 during which there were severe air raids on the locomotive works next to the prison. This was the time when he made his will. Nor did the terror come only at night. He was also tormented during the day. 'Ghastly experiences' often pursued him into the night (*LPP*, 162). At that time, and only then, he thought of suicide, 'not because of an awareness of guilt but because essentially I am already dead. Conclusion, end'. He could shake these experiences off 'only by reciting one hymn after another'; he had the feeling that he was years older, 'and I'm often finding the world nauseating and burdensome'. Prayer is the primary answer to his situation. These texts show us the way to read the rest of Bonhoeffer's literary efforts: they are more the voice of a man at prayer than that of a poet.

The second reason for including the prayers is that in these texts Bonhoeffer takes his place alongside his fellow-prisoners. From the very beginning Bonhoeffer sought to do more than bear his imprisonment in isolation: he was concerned for everyone in the building. We shall also come across this feature later, but it is here that the note is struck. When Bonhoeffer speaks, he is aware of those in the other cells and also has them in mind. He himself may not yet be master of the situation, but his sovereignty is expressed in the way in which he seeks to make things easier for others.

Bonhoeffer always counted the warders as being among his fellow-prisoners. It is clear from his story 'Lance-Corporal Berg' (*LPP*, 253ff) and from his 'Report on Prison Life after One Year in Tegel' (*LPP*, 248ff) that the most brutal warders set the tone for the place: 'the whole building resounds with vile and insulting abuse'. Complaints are useless; sadism and corruption abound. Nevertheless, there were a number of soldiers among the guards with whom Bonhoeffer struck up an intimate relationship over the months, especially during the winter when the prison suffered from air raids. Once the Commandant of Berlin, Bonhoeffer's uncle General Paul von Hase, had enquired after him, his treatment became tolerable and he enjoyed greater freedom. The warders respected him and some even helped him where they could. Some of them even looked to him for protection and consolation. One of them secretly asked him for some 'prayers'. The secret help of understanding men among the older guards also enabled Bonhoeffer to make closer contact with the other prisoners, many of whom were expecting the death penalty. Pastor Dannenbaum and Pastor Poelchau, the prison chaplains, even circulated the 'prayers' among the cells, though this had been strictly prohibited.

Bonhoeffer gave shape to this time of apparently meaningless waiting for release or death by a strict daily routine and fixed times for prayer. The texts we have here are a result of the discipline which he imposed upon himself. He drew strength from the fact that he could not slacken his grip on himself and did not want to do so. However, the 'Prayers for Fellow-Prisoners' are only one instance of his untiring efforts to bring everyone in the sprawling prison of Tegel with whom he was able to make some kind of contact, by his own example, into the field of force from which he drew his own strength. And we shall also see that his prayers included even those who were unknown to him or remained remote from him – the unknowing and the torturers. No service was ever held in Tegel, and Bonhoeffer had no possibility for pursuing such a possibility, but nevertheless something like a Christian community came into being in those surroundings. Five years earlier, when he had been writing the rule for the experimental Finkenwalde community, which had already been banned, Bonhoeffer had stated: 'The physical presence of other Christians is a source of incomparable joy and strength to the believer' (*LT*, 8). Now he found himself more in the position of the apostle Paul, who received his pupil Timothy in prison: still, he could be aware that there were people in the prison who were able to say these prayers with him, whether he knew them or not.

However, these prayers link Bonhoeffer not only with his contemporaries, as is evidenced in their history, but also with the past. That is the third reason which compels us to put the prayers at the beginning of this collection. In the despicable role of a prisoner, Bonhoeffer may have made his life a liturgy, praise from the depths, but in it and through it he was united to and supported by the voices in his ear. In his three prayers there is no mistaking the experience of long Christian tradition; indeed, they are a unique example of the way in which this tradition is taken up in a particular situation. Morning prayers, evening prayers and prayers in times of 'special' distress make up a minimal pattern of daily prayer in monasticism, Lutheranism and pietism, and the verses from long-familiar hymns are given the role of providing an answer to the words of prayer and confirming them through the strength of the community. The words of the individual at prayer are restrained. It would be false to look for originality here. To confront God means to take off all masks. We have a right to assert that this is the atmosphere in which all Bonhoeffer's statements from prison are made. This is his problem when he is writing 'poetry'. He has abandoned the aesthetic dimension, and Rilke's penetrating question, 'Say, poet, what are you doing?', is never far away. This is no time for playing. If there is still beauty in the written words, this beauty comes from the realm of grace. Our first question should not be whether the poems from Tegel lack originality in the artistic sense. They follow the pattern of faith established by the Fathers, which the prisoner finds to be confirmed in his own situation.

Bonhoeffer takes up the tone of the psalms in the Bible: he moves on from confession to praise and thanksgiving and intercession. The keynote is that of confidence in distress, and the address to the Trinity is made quite naturally. Here a man who had made the acquaintance of the depths of anguish and the highest flights of the Spirit, imagination and art, the splendour of earthly glory and the mysteries of theology, puts himself in God's hand like a child. No word indicates any gulf between what he says and who he is. And he prays without giving any sense of urgency, as though he were not a prisoner uncertain how long he had to live. He prays for himself, and as he does so somehow prays for all his fellow-prisoners; indeed, we could repeat the prayers today as though we, many years later, shared his cell. This characteristic of his words forms the basis of all the poems which he has left to us.

THE PAST

'The Past' is the first of the poems that were written in rapid succession during the summer of 1944 in the military prison in the Berlin suburb of Tegel. Bonhoeffer had already been a prisoner for more than a year. True, at this point the prospects for an end to his imprisonment were not completely hopeless, as the authorities had no evidence against him and the hearings were not yet concerned with his personal involvement in plans to overthrow Hitler. Bonhoeffer, accustomed to comfortable middle-class life and with well-developed tastes, who liked to enjoy the best of the gifts of creation, may not have fully got over the shock of confinement in his cell measuring ten feet square, but he had at least accepted his imprisonment and learnt to make use of his everyday intellectual freedom. Nevertheless, he called the content of these verses 'the almost daily accompaniment of my life here' (*LPP*, 319). He felt cut off. There were restrictions on his correspondence and visits always had to be very brief. The necessity of parting hung over every one. Bonhoeffer will have felt this especially when Maria von Wedemeyer, to whom he had become engaged only four months earlier, came to see him. This is a love poem, an act of homage which leaves unnamed the one who was the cause of happiness and sorrow alike.

'The door was slammed;
I hear your steps depart and slowly die away.'

No wonder that this feeling proved so overwhelming. We never hear a single complaint about the difficult conditions in which he had to live. But time was in the balance. Isolation in close confinement can become a symbol for a much more burdensome isolation – that of someone with limited time. Of course, no man knows what the future will bring, and every man is aware that the past is lost time, but the prisoner has a heightened awareness of these things. 'To take leave of others, and to live on past memories, whether it was yesterday or last year (they soon melt into one), is my ever-recurring duty, and you yourself once wrote that saying good-bye goes very much against the grain' (*LPP*, 319). So he wrote to Bethge in his letter of 5 June 1944. The door slamming behind the visitor becomes a symbol of his past life, and after the first five verses of the poem have described the past with the hidden metrical support of an iambic rhythm, a lament begins and continues to the end in an unrhythmical parlando, almost out of breath. He asks why time has to have this character, why what remains is always life which is lost in the past.

No other poem of Bonhoeffer strikes this particular note. As we have already remarked, this prisoner was not one to complain. A Stoic sage of ancient times could also have expressed the wish that he might be granted forgetfulness, since possession was denied him. Bonhoeffer felt this. He draws attention to it in the accompanying letter which he sent to Bethge: 'In this attempt of mine the crucial part is the last few lines' (*LPP*, 319). All day long he had grieved, defiantly and angrily, that a sudden blast of wind snatched away and out of reach the elements of the deepest magic of life as it is lived, the scent of things, the blossoms, greeting and laughter. Like Faust on Easter Eve, who in the end curses even patience, the beating of our heart which keeps corruption at bay, he had even learnt a titanic hate of the fair side of life, simply because it is transitory.

The last verses find an answer from a new perspective. The night has brought the prisoner forgetfulness in sleep and remembrance in dreaming. Waking, he quails before new loss. But his experience will not let him go. He interprets it as a Christian and recognizes the injunction of history: through God the past can be overcome and be made fruitful for the future which he gives.

This is a surprising conclusion. At the end of a poem which represents so abstract a subject as time in pictorial form and is marked by expressions of modern existential distress, the reader feels cheated by expressions which seem to him to be empty clichés. The poet has now given way to the hymn-writer, who can count on the capacity of his congregation to understand figures of speech without their being interpreted. Of course the idea that thanks and repentance, hope for forgiveness and confidence in goodness to come, all play their saving part at the tomb of time, is one which no Christian would dispute and which pagans would accept. But the attempt to express this in poetry does not succeed here. Bonhoeffer himself thought that the last lines were too abrupt. But he should have been suspicious, and not delighted, that 'strangely enough, they came out in rhyme of their own accord'. Reconciliation in rhyme is achieved too quickly after the protest against the cruellest pressures on life which comes pouring out like molten lava. Bonhoeffer was also ill-advised to complain that he had not tried to 'polish' this poem, which came to him 'in a few hours'. The impulsive, spontaneous, expressive, unhindered flow and the harsh changes of rhythm are the features which make it attractive. In the end, polishing would have removed bold, irreplaceable images like those of the face, the hands, the form of life, visible like warm breath in the morning coolness, an image in which the impressions of his young beloved who has just left him after her first visit ('The door was slammed') unite with the theme of the poem.

These verses do not convey a general principle of life, nor do they have universal application. They do not resemble the experience of Prince Buddha on looking at the sick beggar: so it will be with all of us, the decay of our life is sure. Buddha's beggar was one instance of many. Bonhoeffer in prison is himself the instance. We know the life whose departure he laments: the astoundingly rich life of a precocious man, not yet forty, with great musical gifts and sensitivity of spirit. Finally, we can read 'The Past' against the background of the camp at Flossenbürg, where only ten months later Dietrich Bonhoeffer laid down this life which was so precious to him, without being either able or willing to repeat his lament.

In the last book which he gave to us, his uncompleted *Ethics*, he discussed at length his understanding of history. It has the twofold aspect of inheritance and decay. If this poem, completely restricted to personal history, concentrates on decay, in *Ethics* we have a description of the reality of life renewed. The past is not allowed to fade away, as the evening sun sinks into the sea; rather, it is taken up in the awareness that it is not only our destiny, but our debt. In this way it can become our inheritance – in other words, we can profit from it. Once it has been recognized in this way 'one does not seek any eternities from life; one takes what it gives: not everything or nothing, but good and bad, important and unimportant . . . one is content with one's allotted time'. Expressed at greater length, this is also the answer given by the verse with which the poem ends. It is the tersest evidence of Bonhoeffer's trials. And such trials are more severe for those who are not without awareness.

SORROW AND JOY

Now was the time of the incessant Allied air-raids on the
capital, which was already defenceless. Almost a year before the end of the war, half Berlin lay in ruins. However,
Tegel prison was undamaged, and Bonhoeffer learnt that
his parents' house in Charlottenburg was also unscathed.
During these horrific days, doubly helpless as a prisoner, he
was preoccupied with man's helplessness in the face of the
blasts from heaven and in the face of an apparently blind
fate.

This is a text for meditations: inexhaustible, like a view
which becomes transparent for us in an unattended moment;
so to speak, a piece of wisdom, because it became truth in the
experience of the imprisoned poet during the 'laboured
creeping moments of daylight'. Hölderlin's late hymns come
readily to mind: 'Patmos' and 'The Evening of Time'. 'The
Only One' and 'Bread and Wine' – a Sunday for the soul.

Detached formality here swallows up those feelings which
tormented the prisoner and led him, on the day when his
beloved had come to him for the first time and then had to
go again, to lament over the life of which he had been robbed.
Now his gaze is turned away from his own cares towards
man's universal concern, past and present, the stern laws of
life which were making themselves known inexorably to his
generation through the overwhelming event of those days, the
collapse of the middle-class world and of the German dream
of greatness and sovereignty.

Who is speaking here? A Christian, or a descendant of the
Greek seers? Bonhoeffer succeeds in translating his Christian
confession quite naturally in terms of the human cause which
he serves. With their inconspicuous truthfulness and their
restrained progress the words conceal the fact that only a
Christian can speak in this way. Nevertheless, this is an
astonishing theological statement. As we read the poem, we
may be aware of its three dimensions. It is concerned with

the fate of the Germany of the time, which the Germans fail to understand; the fate of the poet himself; and, transcending both, the question which mankind always faces: in all the changes, interruptions, upheavals of our life, whether they are creative or destructive, whether they build us up or tear us apart, do we not feel that we are being put in question? But where does this question come from? In joy as in sorrow something transcendent comes into contact with man, something from beyond the earthly world. He knows both the happiness of joy and his strange malaise after sorrow. The earthly scene is confusing: in devastation we have an inkling of the blessings of nothingness and on the glad arrival of joy we sense the terrifying magnitude of a blessing for which we are too small. Time alone is the judge. Who can bear sorrow for long once it becomes a feature of everyday life? The prisoner has to make his contribution representatively. God visits him in the form of loyalty. But is this only the loyalty of others who are open to God, the loyalty of visitors who are not afraid of 'the monotony of unrelieved unhappiness'? Or does the writer of this verse himself appear at this point?

When Bonhoeffer sent this poem out from the prison, he did not provide a letter to go with it. So it remains a fragment. Not every point in it can be fitted into his situation. However, it does contain ideas on the theme of joy which he set down in other contexts. It is significant that he was in prison when he was concerned to rehabilitate this theme. Only a few weeks after his imprisonment had begun he started to write the history of two families, first in the form of a play and then in the form of a novel, fragments of which still await publication. On 18 November 1943 he wrote to Bethge that he was concerned for a rehabilitation of 'middle-class life as we know it in our own families, and especially in the light of Christianity'(*LPP*, 130). This theme throws up questions which we shall meet again later. Bonhoeffer's literary attempt is an important counterpart to the poems, because it contains a conversation about joy in which

Bonhoeffer again proves himself to be a very individualistic Christian.

'Above all', he makes the representative of the older generation say to the young man, 'beware of speaking lightly of joy and flirting with sorrow. That is contrary to nature, contrary to life, to man as he has been made, living his life as a poor sinner and longing for joy as a small sign of God's good will. It is not as easy as you think to be unhappy, and anyone who really is unhappy doesn't despise and slander the happy. Please . . . none of this wild and arrogant talk about unhappy men and happy pets' (*TP*, 233f).

For all too long it has been supposed that to turn away from the world with a ready eye for sorrow is a Christian virtue. Bonhoeffer forbids us to act in this way. It is not for us to make life beautiful and good (*E*, 185): that is the way it has already been given to us in God's good creation. For the mature man, even life in sorrow is still 'full of sweetness'. But no one should look for sorrow: it is a 'precipitate action' in which God makes contact with us. 'Sorrow comes by itself, or rather from God: we don't have to run after it. To be unhappy is fate, but to want to be unhappy – that's blasphemy, and a serious illness of the soul' (*TP*, 234).

These remarks illuminate the background to the poem, but as we read them we should not think only of the history of Christian piety and misguided strivings for holiness. There is also a contemporary application: these remarks are also concerned with heroism, its cause and its consequences, contempt for creation on the part of an enthusiastic and belligerent youth which allows itself to be made a tool for destroying Germany. If class means anything to Bonhoeffer it means this, that the upper class have the power to make men happy, and this happiness consists in the first place, as he says elsewhere, in 'living alongside other men and getting on with them' (*TP*, 223).

It had been during this year, while he was already wondering which would come first, the overthrow of Hitler or his own arrest, that he had come to know Maria von Wedemeyer, the person with whom he wanted to share his life from now on, with whom he wanted to try his fortune. Bonhoeffer did not see his misfortune or the misfortune of the nation as the end of the world. He had no fanatic belief in his misfortune as others at that time had a fanatic expectation of their death; he experienced the 'hour of devotion' in the devotion of his fiancée, his parents, his friend Bethge and his brother Klaus, who was to follow him to imprisonment and death. What people can give each other when they are together had an 'unearthly radiance' for Bonhoeffer, with his gift for friendship. His sorrow was complete only in solitude. It was already a year since Bonhoeffer had sent his 'wedding sermon' out of the cell and had spoken in it of the joy that people can do so great a thing as to enter into a permanent union (*LPP*, 41). Now he had been engaged to Maria for a year, and they had yet to be able to talk alone together for a single hour. All plans for marriage were postponed 'until the end of the war'. But earlier he had not been aware 'what the warmth which comes from the love of a woman and a family means in the cold air of imprisonment' (ibid.).

The venture of marriage is a step towards affirming the earth and its future, and the longing for earthly happiness 'is justified before God and man' (*LPP*, 42). We could follow Bonhoeffer in putting the point even more sharply: earthly happiness is justified *in* God and *through* God – and this is the key to the present poem. Both sorrow and joy come, apparently 'indistinguishable', from God's hand. What man senses to be 'equally potent in their power and terror', the one and the other, are conjoined through the blessing of this hand. 'God blesses some of his children with joy; he allows everything to succeed for them . . . Other of his children he blesses with sorrow and even martyrdom. God allies himself with both joy and sorrow, in order to guide man on his way and bring him to his goal. Sorrow and joy come to their fulfilment in the blessedness of this goal: we in God and God in us' (*GS* IV, 591). These sentences come from a Pentecost sermon written in his cell during the same year, a few weeks earlier.

There is an obvious question. What gave the prisoner the

strength to set this confession up against the old question of human destiny: Why does this man have joy while I have sorrow? Was this not suggested by the beginning of the poem? We can understand the question, as well as the Orphic style of the poem, once we realize that during this period Bonhoeffer was reading Friedrich Otto's work *The Gods of Greece*, which had been published in 1929. Here for the first time in critical scholarship the author had offered a plausible account of the change from magical religion to the rational Homeric understanding of the world, by refusing to measure the Greek gods by Christian standards. Their power among men is not unlimited; bounds are set to it by the destiny which is inexorably imposed by the fates. The absolute character of destiny is affirmed: the absolute goodness of joy and the absolute evil of sorrow. Bonhoeffer counters this with the result of his discussion: the gentle note in the final verse. Man's own strength can itself reunite what was originally one in God, only to fall apart in human life into opposites, inseparable as absolute joy and 'sorrow's unmistakable features'. For what else would 'transfigured' sorrow be in the loving loyalty of friends but new joy, life trodden through the depths of sorrow, life to which God's 'unspeakably poignant' gifts are again all but 'impossible of just distinction' one from another?

WHO AM I?

The psychologists can do as they please with the foreground. The depths of man escape them. He becomes a riddle to himself. The cell has a bed, a shelf, a stool and a bucket, and there is a hole in the door through which it is possible only to look from the outside in, and not vice versa. Any warder can know at any time where he is with this prisoner. Conditions are as simple as that. Few prisoners in the building are as well known as he is. But he is a contradiction to himself. He knows a man whom the others do not know. And this man cannot be associated with the man whom the warder sees through his hole in the door, the man whom the prisoners meet in the courtyard, in the sick-bay, as an orderly during air-raid warnings.

Dietrich Bonhoeffer added this poem and the one which follows it to one of the great theological letters which still preoccupy scholars today, that of 8 July 1944. It expounds only one of the rich ideas in this letter by means of his own person. It measures the biblical picture of man by the experience of the prisoner. Am I the person they see from the outside, or the one who knows himself to be completely different in his innermost being? 'The Bible does not recognize our distinction between the outward and the inward . . . It is always concerned with the whole man, even where, as in the Sermon on the Mount, the decalogue is pressed home to refer to "inward disposition".' The way in which we enquire about the motive behind the action is therefore also alien to it. 'That a good "disposition" can take the place of total goodness is quite unbiblical. The discovery of the so-called inner life dates from the Renaissance, probably from Petrarch. The "heart" in the biblical sense is not the inner life, but the whole man in relation to God. But as a man lives just as much from "outwards" to "inwards" as from "inwards" to "outwards", the view that his essential nature can be understood only from his intimate spiritual background is wholly erroneous' (*LPP*, 346). Bonhoeffer could discover no psychological explanation for the mutual inter-relationship and interpenetration of the two existences. In the very first months of his imprisonment he had had to accept this in wonderment: 'I often wonder who I really am – the man who goes on squirming under these ghastly experiences in wretchedness that cries to heaven, or the man who scourges himself and pretends to others (and even to himself) that he is placid, cheerful, composed, and in control of himself, and allows people to admire him for it (i.e. for playing the part – or is it not playing a part?)' (*LPP*, 162). The poet recognizes that a psychological examination is no way out of the disjunction, since the very methods of psychology are already governed by the law of disjunction.

The psychology of the situation may well be as the poem describes it, and psychological investigation might feel confident of being able to recognize the reasons. Psychologists believe that they have standards for truth and falsehood, good and evil. However, in his *Ethics* Bonhoeffer had written that for the Christian the simpleness of the new life has dawned in Jesus, which means that good and evil are no longer under man's control (*E*, 31). The Christian has handed back to God the insight which Adam snatched for himself and seeks unity with his will, which is constantly given new life, and not with abstract standards. He may be as complicated as can be in psychological terms – and that was most certainly true of Bonhoeffer; it may often be extremely unclear what God has in store for him or requires of him; his behaviour may often seem mixed both to other people and to himself: the Christian has to surrender even knowledge of himself. Behind everything psychology will uncover a last reflection, a last lack of freedom, a last disjunction, and as we can see, Bonhoeffer worked towards this point without sparing himself. But it is not that. Who would we be if we really knew ourselves? The Christian has firm ground under his feet because God knows him. The unity of our contradictions is to be found only in God.

Bonhoeffer the man is a contradiction of this kind. That we must allow. He accepts that himself. He was very fond of the word 'attitude', and he was fond of talking about the 'free attitude' of faith. In prison he sought to follow the narrow way and to adopt the attitude of 'living every day as if it were our last, and yet living in faith and responsibility as though there were to be a great future' (*LPP*, 15). His life and death showed that this was no façade. He only comes nearer to us when we are aware of the anxieties and the doubts behind this attitude. But he refused to keep asking endless questions about what lay behind. His attitude is to keep it down to a certain level. His attitude gave him the authority which he soon had in the prison.

It was not just the result of Christian discipline, but also the heritage of family tradition and upbringing. The Bonhoeffer family as a whole required certain conduct from its members and maintained it in severe suffering and voluntary sacrifice. We can only marvel at the way in which it was maintained in such hostile circumstances. But is this something that we have to discuss? 'What does one's attitude mean, anyway? . . . I know less than ever about myself, and I'm no longer attaching any importance to it. I've had more than enough psychology, and I'm less and less inclined to analyse the state of my soul. That is why I value Stifter and Gotthelf so much. There is something more at stake than self-knowledge' (*LPP*, 162). So he had written the year before. We can sense how alien he found an age for which human consciousness is the ultimate reality. Did Stifter's *Nachsommer* become this prisoner's dream, just as the novel itself is the vision of a life in freedom and beauty which was denied to Stifter the official, the arbour of the daydream of the downtrodden schoolmaster? Bonhoeffer did not understand his Stifter after the fashion of current literary criticism. What he valued was the way in which Stifter so elegantly objectified the world: he respected concealment and only considered men cautiously from the outside, not from within; curiosity is a stranger to him and he knows the world and men all the better because he was not a psychologist.

That is why this poem is so astonishing. Is not Bonhoeffer doing here precisely what scandalized him so much, giving away his anxiety, his anger, his weariness, his poverty? 'After all, "truthfulness" does not mean uncovering everything that exists. God himself made clothes for men; and that means that *in statu corruptionis* many things in human life ought to remain covered, and that evil, even though it cannot be eradicated, ought at least to be concealed. Exposure is cynical' (*LPP*, 158). But the cynic is preoccupied with disjunction. Bonhoeffer's wonderment at the result of his self-examination can be so penetrating because for him the unity of his person is rooted in God. His reality and his knowledge of our reality is greater than our consciousness. Our weaknesses are true and our strength is true in him. Our questions mock us.

NIGHT VOICES IN TEGEL

With these verses, perhaps the first from June 1944, Bonhoeffer for the first time openly alludes to the cause of his suffering and the reason for the distress of the prisoners. Lying sleepless on his bed, he hears their voices through the walls of his cell like those of ghosts, spirits, witnesses to their unspeakable, bloody struggling and suffering and to unheard-of perversions, while outside the barred window, unreal in its very reality, hour after hour the summer night distils the breath of its utterly different life. It is seen as the symbol of beauty, healing and hope, as the quiet other world which is to be looked for.

During these weeks Bonhoeffer had been reading Dostoevsky's *The House of the Dead*, and like this author he had long found that under the pressure of an exceptional situation which becomes an everyday reality, every aspect of life acquires an over-abundance of meaning. Like Dostoevsky, he had recognized that there is a community between those whom society seeks to put out of action and those who impose and carry out the penalty, a community of degrading compulsion. Here, however, alone in the night, he detaches himself from the everyday life of the prison and lies awake listening to the cries of the souls to whom it brings unutterable torture. First of all he reports what he hears; but then he presents the voices directly in an oratorio, a choral composition in which the voices of those who lament are transformed more and more plainly into those of the accusers. Then midnight ushers in the hour of judgement. Does the thin bell merely proclaim the transition from this day to the next, or does it not rather ring in the new age of the world, when evil will be called evil once more, when the earth will blossom again and man will prosper in freedom?

But the vision fades. The prisoner falls back on his bed. The reality is still darkness. How long will the night continue? Then he hears the night itself speaking and making its own defence. Indeed, night and day have been created good: guilt is the key. The unspeakable could at last be uttered, the wrong done to men in these days of the Hitler regime: the accused accuse the accusers before the throne of God. The choir is silent. No one in prison has freedom of speech. But by night words pass freely through the walls.

Here Bonhoeffer sees the problem which has preoccupied us for so long since the war: the guilt of the innocent, the co-responsibility of the fellow-travellers, the humiliation of the poor in spirit. Hitler involved a whole people, a people with a tradition of piety, the able and the loyal, the lovers of law and order; they had to look upon his perversion of the holy and the true and keep silent; they learned to lie and to adapt themselves to circumstances. However, now in the night they have their voice. The poet seeks to release it; if only they could speak they would necessarily acquit themselves before men.

It may not be inappropriate to suggest that with these verses Dietrich Bonhoeffer paved the way for a spirit which after the war prompted the church to make the so-called Stuttgart Declaration of Guilt (though the negotiations which led up to it contained a great many dubious arguments): 'We accuse ourselves of not having confessed boldly enough, not having prayed faithfully enough, not having believed joyfully enough and not having loved ardently enough.' Those awaiting sentence in Tegel because at some point they have said No to the villain are able to acquit themselves before men, but Bonhoeffer will not do this before God. The chorus can only pray urgently that God will exercise patience, a period of grace, that he will still the storm until new times are ready.

But even as the morning light glimmers through the window set at head height in Bonhoeffer's cell, while a gentle breeze ushers in another summer's day, the prisoner hears the steps of the warder in the corridor. He stops at the next cell. A prisoner is led away: a voice has read out the verdict. 'Control yourself, brother, soon you will have finished it'; the reader will recognize a phrase from the passion story. The one who is left behind has to live for the one who goes before him in suffering.

Bonhoeffer thought that his large-scale poem was 'not too bad'. He did not want to smuggle it out of the prison in the letter. He though that one day 'it will get out', or he wanted to show it to Bethge in person. He still had no suspicion that shortly his situation would get considerably worse; he still hoped that he would not be led away in the greyness of the early morning. In no other poem has he expressed so clearly the thoughts which filled the minds of the prisoners. But he looks forward to the morning. The night will give place and God's will will 'do wonders'. Evil is only a masquerade, and the truth must come to light. He thinks of the time after the war. With that in view, he must use these days fruitfully. While the prison had been resounding with the tumult of the prisoners shut in their cells under a hail of allied bombs, Bonhoeffer may have recalled what he wrote at the end of 1942: 'There remains an experience of incomparable worth, namely, that we have learnt to see the great events of world history for once from below, from the perspective of those who have been shut out, held on suspicion, badly treated; the powerless, the scorned and the oppressed; in short, the sufferers. The all-important thing is that during this time neither bitterness nor envy should have gnawed at our heart, that we should have looked at things great and small, joy and sorrow, strength and weakness, with new eyes; that our insight into greatness, humanity, justice and mercy should have become clearer, freer, more incorruptible, indeed that we should have learnt that personal suffering is a more useful key, a more fruitful principle for discovering the world in contemplation and action than personal good fortune. And it is quite vital that this perspective from below should not just be a matter of taking sides with those who are permanently discontented; rather, we should do justice to life in all its dimensions because of a higher contentment, which has its foundation beyond any perspective, whether from below or from above, and in so doing affirm it' (*GS* II, 441).

We have a jotting from November of the previous year:

'So we must try to keep these experiences in our minds, use them in our work, make them bear fruit and not just shake them off. Never have we been so plainly conscious of the wrath of God, and that is a sign of his grace . . . The tasks that confront us are immense, but we must prepare ourselves for them now and be ready when they come' (*LPP*, 146).

The embarrassment of the nocturnal eavesdropper, the sight and sound of the eloquent yet silent prison with its inmates sleeping a disturbed sleep and its tensely watchful guards, the vision of a night which develops into the night of the world, into judgement and the end of time, coming to its final climax in acknowledgement of the monstrosities and consolation for those doomed to death – this powerful train of thought is authenticated by the existence of the man who has set it down. However, the poem in which it is expressed is less than perfect and its rendering is not without flaw. The beginning, above all, is unfortunate, with its forced rhyme and the recurring clichés. We can grasp the situation, but it is not really embodied in the words. It is as though the poet were still trying out his capabilities. Not until the third strophe does he find the means of expression to match his subject, and the persuasiveness of the poem increases in the same kind of way towards the middle and the end. The simpler the language, the less it looks for striking imagery, the more natural the alternating rhythm becomes, the clearer the mood of the *dies irae* is expressed, the easier it is for us to take part in the exchange between present and future, distress and freedom, misery and glory. This, after all, is Bonhoeffer's concern. We may well ask whether he should have spent more time polishing the poem, or whether perhaps the man who was scholar and pastor, the man involved in the events of his time and the political prisoner serving an indeterminate sentence, did not have the linguistic resources to give poetic expression to a great vision of this kind. However, the dynamic force of this poem and Bonhoeffer's spiritual power are beyond dispute. He can express the suffering, the anguish and the hopes of this section of man's inhuman world as it is to be found in Tegel prison, enfold it in his love and give life to it in such a way that even now it is a warning to us. What have we made of his hopes?

We have certainly done very little with one petition which is expressed here, namely, that after this war it may prove possible for us to construct new ways for the word of God, 'as far as eye can see'. Bonhoeffer made this point on a number of occasions: 'The fact that the horrors of war are now coming home to us with such force will no doubt, if we survive, provide us with the necessary basis for making it possible to reconstruct the life of the nations, both spiritually and materially, on Christian principles' (*LPP*, 146).

He expected of his generation much deeper reflection, a much more thorough assessment of the mistakes and the crimes of the Hitler regime than we in fact provided. On the other hand, he was well aware of the obstacles confronting such a change of direction in Germany where many Christians had in fact accepted Hitler.

CHRISTIANS AND PAGANS

In the briefest possible compass, remarkably impressive by virtue of the slender vocabulary, the parallelism of the lines and the monotony of the three rhymes which recur three times, these three strophes provide a summary of Bonhoeffer's theology. The style invites us to pay attention to the wording, because the words are so very much the same. This is intellectual poetry, which seems to contain no personal note. Yet it tells us what kept Bonhoeffer alive. The middle strophe conveys his special characteristic, the interpretation of Christian belief which still preoccupies us.

The first strophe describes the old way of all religions, which is still very much the fashion: the God who satisfies our desires. Was Ludwig Feuerbach really wrong when he described this God as the product of our wishes? 'Man believes in gods,' he wrote, 'because he has the desire to be happy. He believes in a blessed being because he himself wants to be blessed; he believes in a perfect being because he himself wants to be perfect; he believes in an immortal being because he himself does not want to die.' The Bonhoeffer who wrote this verse regarded religion as 'a historically conditioned and transient form of human self-expression' (*LPP*, 280). The present poem says that it is pagan to regard this conditional form of expression as absolute. But Christians are in the same boat as pagans, in that they know of God only that he wants to be asked for what man needs.

Religion which turns to God and satisfies human desires has three characteristics: it is metaphysical, inward and partial. In other words, it locates God in a beyond. It makes him concerned above all for the salvation of souls and it allows him a special sphere, the sphere of the holy in the world. God is set at the limits of the world, the limits of human knowledge; the almighty is understood as the 'God of the gaps' to make good the gaps in the world, the guardian of man not yet come of age, the counterpart to our impotence. This is what we all rely on, whether we are Christians or pagans. We cast our desires at God's feet. We are deeply religious.

But what, the second strophe asks, if this religion – any religion – has had its day? Is God really wholly other if as far as I am concerned he is simply the power which prevails on earth developed to the ultimate degree, to omnipotence? What if religion is a historically conditioned expression of mankind and in addition if the God who is understood in this way is himself an illusion? 'Man's religiosity makes him look in his distress to the power of God in the world,' wrote Bonhoeffer while he was composing this poem. 'God is the *deus ex machina*. The Bible directs man to God's powerlessness and suffering; only the suffering God can help' (*LPP*, 361).

' "Could you not watch with me one hour?" asks Jesus in Gethsemane. This is a reversal of what the religious man expects from God. Man is summoned to share in God's sufferings at the hands of a godless world.' Bonhoeffer did not have to wait for his imprisonment to rediscover the theology of the cross. From an early stage he was preoccupied with the thought that the Bible does not show us the God whose picture we paint after the measure of our piety, but the God who is weak in order to be able to be strong in his weakness. Prison only confirms this belief. 'That is the foolishness of the revolution of God and its paradoxical character – that just there, where the power of man has lapsed completely, where man knows his own weakness, sinfulness, and consequently the judgement of God upon him, that just there God is already working in grace' (*GS* III, 109, original in English). He wrote these words as early as 1931. This revelation goes against religion and human morality, those two witnesses to God's strength, and the view of the world which has been dominant for so long: it saw God enthroned as the omnipotent deity above a world which he ruled in power, in which his works were so manifest to every man that he was seen to be good and that his goodness and strength could be emulated in moral terms. But men have lost this God and this world. They can no longer find him, and so they have learnt to shape their life without him. They have come of age.

However, a glance at the history of the world shows that God never worked openly for anyone: he was hidden in history. The God of the Bible is to be found on the cross, in the incognito of his weakness and not in the apparent strength of human ideas and social developments. He is not to be found in the crusades or the Utopias and in the first, second and third empires of the conquerors, nor in the glorious heroes or the shining examples of sainthood. God is not the culmination of our ideals and the sum of all power; he really is other, and therefore is weak in this world. He suffers for it, and redeems it through suffering.

This is the God who must be sought. God can only be found in his suffering, says the second strophe, and the last line pictures the task of Christians with unprecedented boldness by playing on the two meanings of the phrase 'stand by', the literal and the metaphorical. In the prisoner's experience, standing by God in his suffering might be the support offered to him by Christians. 'It is not the religious act that makes the Christian, but participation in the sufferings of God in the secular life. That is *metanoia*: not in the first place thinking about one's own needs, problems, sins, and fears, but allowing oneself to be caught up into the way of Jesus Christ, into the messianic event' (*LPP*, 361f).

The suspicions which Bonhoeffer has had for so long are confirmed during his imprisonment; he reads the Bible afresh and discovers the wealth of figures within it, common to all of whom is the fact that they share in the suffering of God in Christ.

But we can only go to God 'in his need' because he is there already and has gone, continues to go, 'to all men in their need'. Neither the efforts of pagan and Christian religious striving nor the faith which takes as its support the Jesus of the garden of Gethsemane, the witness to a God who really comes down into our world, and by whom we have to stand, offer a method by which Pastor Bonhoeffer could bring God home either to the poor screaming men in prison or to us.

There is no technique for getting the better of the situation in Tegel, even for the poet himself. His profoundest struggle during the eighteen months he was in Tegel was to live completely as a sufferer among the sufferers, in a world which no longer offers religious help, and to confess the real presence of the apparently absent God, not through words but in his life. This was the only way that he believed to be still open to Christians. But he did not describe it further and he was unable to draw out its consequences for the church. He only knew one thing, and that is expressed in the last line: at all points we are directed towards forgiveness. And this has come about in a much more comprehensive way than the religions and confessions, the pietists and the liberals, the faithful and the godless ever believe to be possible; God has already distributed the bread in the sacrament of the cross on Golgotha.

STATIONS ON THE ROAD TO FREEDOM

At a stroke, the situation had become very critical for
Bonhoeffer and most of his friends: the revolt, planned for
so long, and on which he had pinned all his own hopes, had
been attempted on 20 July 1944 and had collapsed after a
few hours. To begin with, Hitler intended to make short
shrift of all the conspirators, whom he thought to be only a
small misguided clique. However, the so-called Zossen files,
which were discovered on 20 September, went on to show
that the group was much larger than had hitherto seemed
likely. So Hitler postponed the death sentences and ar-
ranged extensive investigations.

Dietrich Bonhoeffer had been working in the sick-bay when
he heard on the radio the news of the attempted overthrow
and the first arrests. Over the following weeks the Gestapo
spread their net closer and closer to him. After the discovery
of the files he made contact with his family through a guard
at Tegel and planned his escape. However, when his brother
Klaus was arrested he changed his plans. On 8 October he
was transferred from Tegel into the basement prison at
Gestapo headquarters in the Prinz Albrecht Strasse. His
position was now completely different, and conditions in
the prison were much more severe. He was to remain here
for four months. Harsh interrogation was to clarify his part
in the plans for the overthrow. Five members of his family
were now in prison.

It is necessary to be aware of this if we are to put following
poems in context. They were all written after the situation
had deteriorated to such a degree and after the hope which
Bonhoeffer and his friends had cherished for so long had also
faded, namely that at the last minute the attempt against
Hitler would prevent the downfall of Germany. From 20
July Bonhoeffer could no longer hope for freedom; this was
now something 'which here remains hidden'. So what he
now said in these four verses, each of six hexameters, without

a word too many or a word too few, was nothing new for him. He simply had to remember what had always been the heart of what he had sought to put into practice in his ethics. Now the hour of trial had come, and now more clearly than at any time since his arrest eighteen months before, there had opened up the other necessary road to freedom which he had been shown.

His resolve as a Christian not only to be a spectator of disaster but also to set out with others on the course of liberation through action had already been prepared for by his idea of faith, his ethics and his understanding of the world. It was impossible for him to remain inactive. To act also involves a judgement. Being a Christian is put to the test in our secular action in the godless world, not in retreat to a sacred sphere. The Christian acts in freedom and as a free man. Bonhoeffer said what that meant in his work and showed it in his life. In the last resort, however, freedom is a costly goal which is difficult to learn.

The first strophe expresses the human presupposition. Freedom is not doing as one pleases. Man is not free over against himself. In *The Cost of Discipleship*, a book which in prison he was now to call dangerous (*LPP*, 401), because it might prompt a retreat from the world, Bonhoeffer was fond of talking of the 'discipline of obedience'. Now, as we have seen, he preferred to talk of an 'attitude'. In a new work for which he made a sketch during these weeks, he wrote that the model for man which is based on the humanity of Jesus would again have to have a place in the church after the collapse of Germany.

It seems as though a monk is talking here. In fact Bonhoeffer sometimes acknowledged his longing for a monastic life, and while he still had the opportunity sought to build up a community of brothers with a common discipline, joining together in withdrawing from an unstructured life. The beginning of the freedom of a Christian man is for him to be a servant of all things. Here Bonhoeffer is also talking of his experience in prison. As we have already pointed out, in this situation he made time and found strength to give a great deal to many people by thinking, writing and acting, through an organized and disciplined way of life. Now for the last time he was to make the point once again: the Christian must not hold his life cheaply.

We can achieve freedom in action and in suffering. Both are ambivalent, especially action. Restriction is the criterion. Our hands are tied in suffering and our thoughts in action. Throughout his life Bonhoeffer had been preoccupied with the relationship between action and thought. What action bestows freedom? This poem looks back on the considerations which Bonhoeffer expressed in his *Ethics*: free action is impossible for the rational man and the ethical fanatic, for the virtuous or the conscientious, for the one who does his duty or the one who thinks that he is free to come to a responsible decision. Freedom will only 'welcome your spirit with joy' if you leave the decision about good and evil, right and wrong actions, about yourself in your own actions, to God. But, as we read in the last jottings to find their way out from his cell, all genuine experience of God derives from Jesus, 'Jesus who is there only for others . . . Faith is participation in this being of Jesus from freedom from oneself, being there for others maintained till death' (*LPP*, 381).

The resolve to act is thus made possible through the belief that judgement on the action will be made only by God. Helplessness can be content with the belief that God will perfect weakness in glory. To accept suffering in this way is to be free. But all these are marginal notions, and certainty has to be sought again and again. Otherwise suffering would not be suffering. Freedom is not a possession. Only for a moment can the sufferer touch it blissfully; then he gives it back to the God from whom it comes.

And yet the prisoner, who finds himself in this situation, goes on to add one last stage. He sees the approach of the day of his ultimate loss of freedom, when he whom the other prisoners always regarded as a squire because he could step so cheerfully and so freely from his cell wiil be treated as an object that has to be destroyed. This ultimate loss of freedom, death, the incompatible, will prove his supreme freedom.

On this day he will find what he has sought for so long.

In these lines a note is struck which is new to Christianity. The nobility of this man's disposition is combined with a humility which is utterly open. A bold theological insight, gained with difficulty and hard to grasp, is here expressed in words so simple that they cannot fail to move. Here is the summary of an entire life the consummation of which is in sight. One who has stood 'in the storm of events' has found the eye of the hurricane where stillness prevails. Talking of death brings joy. The one who is to depart offers guidance. The one who has failed goes to meet his God. Freedom is granted to the one who wanted to bring freedom. Bonhoeffer thought that a necessary connection would be seen here. For this is the point at which the decision is made whether human action is a matter of faith or not: 'whether we understand our suffering as an extension of our action and a completion of freedom or not' (*LPP*, 375).

THE FRIEND

If the previous poem spoke of freedom, here we have freedom itself. The previous poem expressed the constraints on the free Christian man in a highly stylized form within a narrow compass; this poem describes the royal freedom of the prisoner by many concrete examples, in free verse, with a wealth of strophes and a cheerful flow of dactyls. Here is creation without the fall. The theologian seems to be completely silent. Here is acceptance of the world which the sufferer is learning to renounce. Here is a man endowed with the grace which has so seldom disclosed itself even to the Christian man, although he is well aware of it: 'the freedom of a lightsome, daring, trusting spirit' as well as the earnestness of his cause. That, says the poet who is writing about friendship, is freedom, the fruit and the blossom. But in the poem he himself becomes the theme.

Here before us we have a Bonhoeffer who has been in prison for eighteen months. The daily routine, the endless interrogation, the taunts of the guards, the newly dawning certainty that the doors will never open for him again – none of this can take away the magic of his personality. As the poems also show us, he was blessed with many gifts. In his youth he wondered whether he should not devote his life to music, and he was always a good pianist. There is abundant testimony to the indomitable, spontaneous charm of his conversation. He seemed to have friends everywhere. This poem is addressed to one particular friend, Eberhard Bethge, who since his marriage to Bonhoeffer's niece was now one of the family. It was written for Bethge's birthday, and is therefore deeply personal, as is underlined still further by the last two anxious strophes, set apart from the rest of the poem by the different metre in which they are written. However, at the same time it is Bonhoeffer's testament for all his friends, about the meaning and value and beauty of friendship, this 'cornflower in the field' of the good gifts of God. It is the nature of friendship that it grows in freedom, un-protected and 'in glad confidence'.

Bonhoeffer had already spoken about the connection between friendship and freedom at the beginning of the year in a letter to Renate and Eberhard Bethge. Friendship does not appear among the ordinances of creation as they are to be found in traditional dogmatics – Bonhoeffer preferred to speak of God's four mandates for the world. The mandate of work gives rise to comradeship, that of marriage to its special partnership; and even in the mandate of the state and authority friendship is an alien body. The church has developed brotherhoods and sisterhoods and yet for a long time has found no home for friendship. Friendship, wrote Bonhoeffer, belongs in the sphere of freedom. Christians have to rediscover its claim as they have to rediscover freedom itself.

In teaching Christians once again to distinguish between the man who hands himself over freely to God's will and the man concerned with legalistic ethics, Bonhoeffer wants a place to be found for friendship in the church (*LPP*, 193). Friendship is not 'necessary', but a gift made 'in the free pleasure and the free desire of the spirit'. It has its existence alongside what is necessary, alongside the first three mandates, 'marriage, work and the sword'. But freedom is necessary; friendship lives by virtue of its claim on freedom, and 'I believe that within the sphere of this freedom friendship is by far the rarest and most priceless treasure' (ibid.). Schiller's verse 'He who has known the great fortune of being bosom friend to friend' shows very well that friendship is at the same time both joy and achievement, play and destiny, freedom and necessity.

However, in contrast to the poems which precede it and follow it, this composition is not concerned with abstract ideas. It does not express theories about friendship, but conjures it up in the reminiscences of this one friendship with the friend who also edited his work, who stimulated and evoked it, followed its course, collected it and interpreted it, and who soon afterwards was himself imprisoned.

Adventures of the spirit, the laborious growth of work, preoccupied this friend: at one point he seeks trust, seeks to lay himself completely open, to be given ungrudging recognition and rigorous criticism, 'counsel from one who is earnest in goodness and faithful in friendship'. That is the theme of those strophes. One could interpret them word by word through long accounts from the history of this friendship, and perhaps one day the friend who still survives will do this, when time has elapsed to make the attempt possible and before the fragrance of the cornflower has vanished.

A third aspect of these verses can also be noted. The spirit of this friendship and of what Bonhoeffer understood to be friendship in general is connected with the élitist traits which we have already noted elsewhere in this poetry. The background to it and the presuppositions for it are to be found in the history of the Bonhoeffer family and in the contents of the fragments of a play and a novel which Bonhoeffer wrote. To talk here of the game of friendship does not mean that the word is played out. The basis for it is a shared delight in increased knowledge brought about by a shared life, and a growing awareness of being there for the other person in the spirit and as a companion, through action and through patience. 'There is hardly anything that can make one happier than to feel that one counts for something with other people. What matters here is not numbers, but intensity. In the long run, human relationships are the most important thing in life; the modern "efficient" man can do nothing to change this, nor can the demigods or lunatics who know nothing about human relationships. God uses us in his dealings with others. Everything else is very close to *hubris* ... That certainly doesn't mean undervaluing the world of things and practical efficiency. But what is the finest book, or picture, or house, or estate, to me, compared to my wife, my parents, or my friend? One can, of course, speak like that only if one had found others in one's life. For many today man is just a part of the world of things, because the experience of the human simply eludes them. We must be very glad that this experience has been amply bestowed on us in our lives' (*LPP*, 386).

Only the one who is himself a man can have experience of the human, and only the one who can be a friend can win friends. This is what countless contemporaries reported of Dietrich Bonhoeffer. Bonhoeffer was a theologian with great gifts. Our generation has yet to catch up with all his thinking. But the secret of his work was that he never took up questions which were only theoretical questions for him. No matter what he did, learning and studying, free or in prison, he was the man who turned towards men. He was able to enjoy himself and wanted to do so, but he did not want any enjoyment that he could not share with his men. He felt that a 'professorial' existence was impermissible. Right up to the end he had about him the air of freedom. Another friend put it this way: 'His appearance was imposing but not elegant; his voice high but rich; his formulations were laborious, not brilliant. Perhaps it was here that we met a quite single-hearted, or in the words of the gospel, a "single-minded" man. Never did I discover in him anything low, undisciplined, mean. He could be relaxed, but he never let himself go. He detested binding men to himself: perhaps for that very reason so many were drawn to him' (Albrecht Schönherr in *I Knew Dietrich Bonhoeffer*, p. 126).

THE DEATH OF MOSES

In a letter quoted by Eberhard Bethge which has not in fact been preserved, we read of Bonhoeffer's fear that the theme of 'The Death of Moses' would have been too 'explosive' for him had he not written on it in verse. The correspondence of that period was burnt, as Bethge's arrest was imminent.

The death of Moses is described in the last chapter of the Pentateuch, which the Jews call the Torah. Moses had led his people into the wilderness from their captivity in Egypt and had guided them in patience, faithfulness and love. He had shown them the will of God as expressed in his law and the Book of the Covenant, and had made them the sanctuary of the tabernacle and ordered their sacrificial worship. He had come forward as mediator between the apostate people and their God and had finally led them as far as the promised land. Now he stands on Mount Nebo, overlooking the Jordan valley, and gazes on the celebrated land of Canaan which they have been promised, with its rivers and palm trees. 'And the Lord said to him. "This is the land of which I swore to Abraham, to Isaac and to Jacob, 'I will give it to your descendants.' I have let you see it with your eyes, but you shall not go over there." So Moses the servant of the Lord died there.' Others will carry on his work, and his grave will remain unknown.

Dietrich Bonhoeffer was always suspicious of any attempt to move too quickly from the Old Testament to the New. He felt close to the Old Testament because it understands redemption in historical terms and does not set it in the beyond, the other side of the boundary of death. As he recognized his own career in this poem, in the symbol of Moses, he was certain that his suffering generation would not allow themselves to be comforted by the thought of heaven. The new land is not a land beyond time; it is the other side of the Jordan which lies before our eyes. And in modern terms the Jordan means the end of the war, the end of the 'villain', the end of the kingdom of lies, of death and of prisons.

We cannot disguise the fact that the poem is unsuccessful. We do not know the reason why. Bonhoeffer did not have the resources to carry it off. He falls victim to the constraint of the harsh metre with its five feet of trochees and the strong rhymes. The poem has a beat, but neither rhythm nor melodious language. It never sets us on fire; all the way through we cannot note more than minor felicities. Had Bonhoeffer succumbed to the monotony of his imprisonment? Were his spiritual powers maimed? That would be quite understandable, and it is out of place for us to play the Beckmesser here. He would never have allowed it to be published, and it is the only one of his poems which was not included in the great collection of his writings from prison. It is to be found complete in the fourth volume of his *Collected Writings*; here we have included only the last of its ninety couplets.

Still, it seems important that we should investigate what this poem has to say. Its statements are important as a farewell. We find the comparison difficult: the aged Moses, one hundred and twenty years old, as the Bible says, and Bonhoeffer, thirty-eight and in the prime of life. Did Bonhoeffer feel old? Along with this poem in September 1944 he sent his friend Bethge a discussion of the concept of the future (*LPP*, 398). He wished that we might have the courage to speak about it in concrete terms. But his picture, too, is only that of a Utopia. And had he survived, he would hardly have found himself in a 'garden', in God's kingdom of grace, justice, truth, peace, tranquillity and faith. No one will ever be able to measure what blessings we would have been given had Dietrich Bonhoeffer been allowed to tread the promised land of peace for Europe.

The poem depicts the path of the aged Moses. 'His eye was not dim, nor his natural force abated,' as the Bible tells us. He acknowledges his own lack of faith and praises God's faithfulness towards his people; he thanks God for granting him a proud, free death on the mountain and celebrates the promised land at his feet, 'God's vineyard, freshly bathed in dew.' He understands his death as a punishment for the faithlessness of his people. This is the theme of representativeness. Bonhoeffer had written: 'We are certainly not Christ; we are not called on to redeem the world by our own deeds and sufferings, and we need not try to assume such an impossible burden. We are not lords, but instruments in the hand of the Lord of history; and we can share in other people's sufferings only to a very limited degree' (*LPP*, 14).

Looking towards the change which would free his people but which he would not live to see, the poet stands in Moses' place:

Enough that I have borne its shame and sin

and seen salvation – now I need not live.

He has done all that a Christian can: 'We are not Christ, but if we want to be Christians, we must have some share in Christ's large-heartedness by acting with responsibility and in freedom when the hour of danger comes, and by showing a real sympathy that springs, not from fear, but from the liberating and redeeming love of Christ for all who suffer' (ibid.).

Responsibility for all, suffering with all, a future hope for all, a solitary, lonely death for himself, held back by God in the distress of the old world with the prospect of a new world just in sight – this is his fate. Bonhoeffer sees Moses as Christ and at the same time as a possible way of understanding his own career. The 'veil of death' has been spread round about, but freedom is imminent. God's anger has struck, but his grace brings deliverance. For the believer he makes bitterness sweet. The meaning of death is the liberation that it brings. He will not see the new land, but he is allowed to know that it is there. The only reward for the labourer is that others will complete his work.

Bonhoeffer may have come to associate himself with this figure of Moses during his time of doubt. Such times were rare with him. We do not see any change of tone or mood in his letters after 20 July 1944. Even while he is in the Gestapo prison he does not complain; his letters are cheerful and matter of fact; he is concerned about his friends, his relatives and the German people, but never about himself. He had thought before about the time which had now come: 'What would I do if I knew that I had only four to six months to live?' he had written four years earlier. At that time he had replied: 'I think that I would try to go on teaching theology as before, and to preach often' (GS IV, 7). This is what he tried to do now. He produced a sketch for a new book. He preached about Moses on Mount Nebo. And he composed this message in verse. Otherwise, as we have seen, he felt that it would have been too explosive.

Did he intend there to be a concealed political statement in this theme? Was the wandering of the people in the wilderness now over? Was there an end to the time of hostility to God, revolt, apostasy, unbelief? Was his vision so bold as to suggest that like Moses, and indeed like Christ, the righteous man can accept death on behalf of his people, as a punishment and an expiation? Did he want to tell us one last time, in the Gestapo basement, his last mountain in the wilderness, that against all our expectations God is faithful to the very end?

Stay, hold my nerveless hands, let fall my staff;
thou faithful God, prepare for me my grave.

JONAH

There are four aspects to the language of this poem, the last to have been written in Tegel. First, it is a masterpiece of contemporary application, concentration and exposition. With a succinct earnestness which defies description, Bonhoeffer offers an interpretation of the biblical story and at the same time touches on the history of the countless attempts not only of scholars, but also of the Jewish and Christian communities, to interpret the text of Jonah. Third, it proclaims that the prophet's message is a word for the church at the time of a dawn of a new era in Europe. And finally here, as in all the previous poems, Dietrich Bonhoeffer bears witness to himself. Now as he writes, probably on 5 or 6 October 1944, he reflects upon his own position and his own career as it has been and as it will be, with a seriousness that is heightened even further. It is impossible to plumb all these four levels. We must ask the reader to be content with the allusions made here. In the last resort, every great poem eludes interpretation. Our task can only be to elucidate some of the ciphers behind which the reader will find the deepest meaning of the verses.

In the story of Jonah, so oddly included among the books of the 'minor prophets' in the Old Testament, the universalist and ecumenical dimension of Judaism comes to light. Here is a refutation of the prejudiced view that Israel seeks to keep its election to itself. This is the story of the man who does not want God to give salvation to everyone, the story of the Pharisee who accuses Jesus of seeking out the cheats and the prostitutes, the story of the church which is intent on itself instead of bearing witness to the love of God for the godless world in the godless world. Bonhoeffer rediscovered himself in the first chapter of this precious legend: the prophet has been commanded by God to preach repentance to the sinful city of Nineveh, where people 'do not know their right hand from their left'. But Jonah refuses, and flees from God's voice. He goes from Mount Tabor, where he lives, to Jaffa, by the sea. There he finds a ship bound for Spain, in the opposite direction from Nineveh in Assyria, where he had been ordered to go. Now, however, he learns that it is vain to flee before God.

Bonhoeffer takes up only this part of the story. He presupposes its beginning and its sequel. Jonah sees the storm as God's word to him. Again he tries to refuse. He goes down into the hold and sleeps. Is not God almighty? He will calm even the savage sea. After all, he made it. All will turn out well. But the crew reprove him. How could he flee before such a God? In terror of death they ask what is going to happen. Jonah offers himself as a victim. According to ancient ideas of magic, the force of nature could be tempered by a sacrifice. The poem does not mention that Jonah is saved and that after resisting yet again he finally brings his commission to a successful conclusion in Nineveh.

Presumably Bonhoeffer abandoned his carefully prepared plans for escape on the very day on which he composed this poem. In contrast to earlier expectations, his escape would have put his parents and others among his nearest relatives in acute danger, along with their families and friends. They too were engaged in opposition to the Hitler regime. Furthermore, it was at this point that his brother Klaus had been arrested for his involvement in the conspiracy against Hitler. So Bonhoeffer gave up all hope of deliverance. It was by no means presumptuous for him to see himself in the picture of Jonah, who offered his life for others. He is Jonah among the godless who prove to be more god-fearing than he, the pious man, who must be made to see that the love of God goes far beyond the limits of the church. And again, as in the poem about Moses, he is concerned with the idea of representativeness. The terror of the sea, the 'gods provoked to anger', the forces of the time 'unchained in sudden fury', call for the guilty one. Jonah recognizes that it is his failure, his disobedience which has led God to allow this disaster. He acknowledges the fact. He accepts the blame. He offers up his life. And they cast him away to destruction. 'We have not loved faithfully enough', the church was to say only a year later, in the Stuttgart Declaration of Guilt. Bonhoeffer has now already said that in a cryptic way, the only way possible at the time, although he proved his active love with long imprisonment and was to prove it further with his death.

So this poem must also be read as a word to the church. He had always been complaining over the years that its horizons were too narrow, so he had to show it the way. He had to go where the storm was raging, to risk his life, to refuse the invitation to stay in America, where he would have been warmly welcomed, at the time of danger. He had to take part in the attempt against Hitler, above all by his dangerous journeys; he felt that the Christian should stand outside where 'they cried aloud in fear of death'. Even where the church of his time had protested, it had thought chiefly of itself and its pastors in prison, and much too little about Jews and political prisoners.

This connection becomes clear if we remember that from earliest times Christians have read the first part of the Jonah story as a prefiguration of baptism. Baptism immerses men, like Jonah, in the waters of death, so that they will once again be raised up to life, just as by a miracle Jonah did not die, but was conveyed and set on dry land by a 'great fish'. Six months earlier, in May, Bonhoeffer had sent a sermon from prison to his friend Bethge and his niece Renate on the occasion of the baptism of their first child, since he could not be there to deliver it in person. It led him to survey at length what they had done together and to look ahead to the future, while at the same time making a detached yet deeply committed comment on the present situation. In this context he found words of harsher prophecy to say about the church than he had ever used before. To keep the imagery, is the church not Jonah sleeping in the hold?

'Our church, which has been fighting in these years only for its self-preservation, as though that were an end in itself, is incapable of taking the word of reconciliation and redemption to mankind and the world. Our earlier words are therefore bound to lose their force and cease, and our being

Christians today will be limited to two things: prayer and righteous action among men. All Christian thinking, speaking, and organizing must be born anew out of this prayer and action' (*LPP*, 300).

Bonhoeffer's theme is not that Jonah is saved, but that he saves. The miracle can happen because Jonah acknowledges that there is reason for God's anger. Among those who 'cry in fear of death' and whose bodies 'strain' at the last straw – scenes with which Bonhoeffer was confronted every day – he stands as the one to whom this story relates, and so he can interpret it. Someone must be guilty, men ask 'among men'. The guilty one is the one who knows the will of God. No one can say in advance whether the sea really will 'stand still' if a man ventures the new way of handing himself over unprotected. Not to know what will happen next is an essential part of the venture. Because God will not remain in Tabor, but seeks out Nineveh, Bonhoeffer had to take the risk of being cast into the sea along with the pious children of this world, the conservatives and the socialists, who at that time were called a clique of conspirators, criminals and traitors.

POWERS OF GOOD

The verses which bring this collection to an end also bring to an end what Dietrich Bonhoeffer wanted to say on the eve of the last year of his life. For a long time now they have been included in books used in German schools; they have often been set to music, and there can be few Christians of our generation in the Protestant churches who do not know them. There can be no question of their stature: they are simple yet profound, prompted by utmost turmoil, yet running their tranquil course in the strength of a manly hope. The seven strophes express gratitude, readiness for sacrifice, the steadfast acceptance of suffering and renewed purpose. What makes the poem one of the most precious treasures of spiritual experience and one of the most important texts of Christian prayer is the quite natural assurance to be found here, the belief in God's protection even in these 'evil days'. Indeed, now Bonhoeffer seems to be more certain of this than ever before. Here, we can see the simple yet wide-ranging symbols of the faith which continually sustained him in his theological concerns, as he boldly pressed ever onwards in that extremely learned conversation between heart and head which was maintained literally until the last weeks of his life: light in darkness, a cry from the depths, the salvation of souls in terror, the high triumph-song resounding down the ages, thanksgiving for the cup of suffering, all this Nevertheless, this Yes in the No of our earthly existence. In the end it is all very simple. That is the mark of all that is great. By this we can assess the spiritual stature of what he develops to such an impressive degree.

What are the powers of good which are mentioned in the first and last strophes, and which form the presupposition for all that is said in between? Anyone can understand the phrase, just as anyone can understand all the words in this poem. At the beginning of his career as a Christian and a thinker, Bonhoeffer would have said 'God'. Now he wants to give this word content. Abstract concepts will not do. He has learnt this much as he has worked with them. In thinking of his goodness, he does not want to run away from these experiences.

Just earthly things occur to him when he begins to talk of the powers of good and of God's goodness which continues to surround him at every turn. Think of what is to come: the basement of the Gestapo prison in Prinz Albrecht Strasse in December and January and the terrible interrogations; his last birthday on 4 February, the final departure, the end of all contacts with the outside world, Berlin in ruins, the evacuation on 7 February, the time in Buchenwald for another two months, the wrong route of the guards into the Danube valley, where there was even a glimpse of freedom, and then the abrupt end, the emergency court and execution in the grey morning light of 9 April 1945. The camp doctor described the scene: he had never seen a man die like that, not in fifty years. Just earthly things occurred to him when he spoke of God's goodness. He was glad to get to know so many interesting prisoners on the last journey. He carried on endless conversations, learnt Russian from a young Russian prisoner and prayed with them. Payne Best, an English prisoner, later wrote of him: '. . . he always seemed to diffuse an atmosphere of happiness, of joy in every smallest event in life, and of deep gratitude for the mere fact that he was alive. He was one of the very few men I have ever met to whom his God was real and ever close to him' (*DB*, 823).

In one of the few letters to his fiancée Maria von Wedemeyer which have been published, in fact the last letter which he wrote to her shortly before his last Christmas, he describes the 'powers of good'. The words he uses are not theological. The powers of good are to be described in terms of our own life. God is here among us. 'You, the parents, all of you, the friends and students of mine at the front, all are constantly present to me. Your prayers and good thoughts, words from the Bible, discussions long past, pieces of music, and books, – all these gain life and reality as never before. It is a great invisible sphere in which one lives and in whose reality there is no doubt. If it says in the old children's song about the angels: "Two, to cover me, two, to wake me," so is this guardianship, by good invisible powers in the morning and at night, something which grown-ups need today no less than children. Therefore you must not think that I am unhappy. What is happiness and unhappiness? It depends so little on the circumstances; it depends really only on that which happens inside a person. I am grateful every day that I have you, and that makes me happy' (*LPP*, 419).

The difference lies in whether one says it beforehand or afterwards. Certainly, because we may often have pious feelings, we often confuse our happiness with God and God with our happiness. It is easy to do that or to say it because the sun is shining, without having either come to know God or really taking our happiness to heart. Earlier in his career Bonhoeffer as a theologian had presented all the arguments for and against the great Schleiermacher, who had lent so much support to this confusion! Most of us find that our thinking moves in the opposite direction: at the beginning we live for our day and call our love God and God love, as long as he does not deprive us of anything. Then in our old age we again move him to the boundaries, because we want to be sure to go where the path leads. And if that does not work out, we give up altogether and become cynical. Bonhoeffer showed us another way. The hotter hell became, the more sure he was of the strength of the powers of good; moreover, he believed that they are not outside somewhere, but here. They are near to us and bear the same name as everything that he felt to be a good gift.

This he read in his Old Testament, and he never wanted it to be set on a lower level than the New Testament. The Old Testament taught him how seriously earthly things are intended and how seriously they are to be taken. God's purpose for us is happiness. He brings it to us through his blessing. Men may make use of it. 'Blessing means to put one's hand on something and to say: despite everything, you belong to God. This is what we do with the world, which brings us such suffering. We do not abandon it, reject it, condemn it, despise it; we summon it to God, we give it hope, we lay our hand on it and say: God's blessing be upon you, may he renew you. Be blessed, world which has been created by God, world which belongs to your Creator and Redeemer' (*GS* IV, 596). Earthly life is to be had in the fullness of time. There is life only for those who cannot but 'think of the past'.

Bonhoeffer was a grateful man, and in this respect he was already rich. In his ear resounded the voice of history, 'their universal paean, in thy praise'. He did not forget the fullness of all his brief years, nor anything of what he had been given. That means that he did not forget God. The powers of good were not just the destination of his momentary prayers, but the light in which he breathed.

'We have received God's blessing in joy and in suffering. And the one who has been blessed in this way cannot but hand on this blessing. Indeed, he himself must be a blessing, wherever he is. The world can only be renewed on an impossible basis; and this impossible basis is the blessing of God' (ibid.).

W. H. AUDEN

FRIDAY'S CHILD

In memory of Dietrich Bonhoeffer, martyred at Flossenbürg,
9 April 1945

He told us we were free to choose
But, children as we were, we thought –
'Paternal Love will only use
　　Force in the last resort

On those too bumptious to repent.'
Accustomed to religious dread,
It never crossed our minds He meant
　　Exactly what He said.

Perhaps He frowns, perhaps He grieves,
But it seems idle to discuss
If anger or compassion leaves
　　The bigger bangs to us.

What reverence is rightly paid
To a Divinity so odd
He lets the Adam whom He made
　　Perform the Acts of God?

It might be jolly if we felt
Awe at this Universal Man;
(When kings were local, people knelt)
　　Some try to, but who can?

The self-observed observing Mind
We meet when we observe at all
Is not alarming or unkind
　　But utterly banal.

Though instruments at Its command
Make wish and counterwish come true,
It clearly cannot understand
  What It can clearly do.

Since the analogies are rot
Our senses based belief upon,
We have no means of learning what
  Is really going on,

And must put up with having learned
All proofs or disproofs that we tender
Of His existence are returned
  Unopened to the sender.

Now, did He really break the seal
And rise again? We dare not say;
But conscious unbelievers feel
  Quite sure of Judgement Day.

Meanwhile, a silence on the cross
As dead as we shall ever be,
Speaks of some total gain or loss,
  And you and I are free

To guess from the insulted face
Just what Appearances He saves
By suffering in a public place
  A death reserved for slaves.

W. H. Auden met Bonhoeffer at the home of Richard
Niebuhr during 1939, on Bonhoeffer's visit to America. At the
time Bonhoeffer was thirty-three years old. This poem may
express in poetic language some of the content of the theological discussion which they had at the time. The reference
to Friday's child, loving and giving, seems to reflect an

important side to Bonhoeffer's character. The poem itself is enigmatic, difficult and ambivalent, with Auden's characteristic ironical detachment and his brilliant disregard for grammar and the obvious meaning. Bonhoeffer certainly never wrote with this kind of bleakness. But the poem does highlight for us the contradiction and the questions which he posed to those who talked with him. The conclusion is prophetic.

The poems included in this volume were originally published as follows:

Prayers for Fellow-Prisoners, *LPP*, 139-43
The Past, *LPP*, 320-3
Sorrow and Joy, *LPP*, 334f.
Who am I?, *LPP*, 347f.
Night Voices in Tegel, *ILP*, 51-9
Christians and Pagans, *LPP*, 348f.
Stations on the Road to Freedom, *LPP*, 370f.
The Friend, *LPP*, 388-91
The Death of Moses, *GS* IV, 619f.
Jonah, *LPP*, 398f.
Powers of Good, *LPP*, 400f.

DB   Eberhard Bethge, *Dietrich Bonhoeffer:* Man of Vision, Man of Courage, Harper & Row, Publishers, Inc. 1970

E   *Ethics* (based on the arrangement of the sixth German edition), Macmillan Publishing Co., Inc. 1965

GS   *Gesammelte Schriften* (six volumes), Christian Kaiser Verlag 1965-74

ILP   *I Loved This People,* John Knox Press 1965

LPP   *Letters and Papers from Prison,* The Enlarged Edition, Macmillan Publishing Co., Inc. 1972

LT   *Life Together,* Harper & Row, Publishers, Inc. 1954

TP   *True Patriotism,* edited by Edwin H. Robertson, Harper & Row, Publishers, Inc. 1973